DO YOU BELIEVE WHAT

GOD SAYS ABOUT YOU?

STEPHEN VIARS

HARVEST HOUSE PUBLISHERS
EUGENE. OREGON

Do You Believe What God Says About You?
Copyright © 2022 by Stephen Viars
Published by Harvest House Publishers
Eugene, Oregon 97408
www.harvesthousepublishers.com

ISBN 978-0-7369-8442-3 (pbk)
ISBN 978-0-7369-8443-0 (eBook)

Library of Congress Control Number: 2021937929

To my mother Wanda,
who helped me to shape my identity
by regularly pointing me to Christ and his Word.

Contents

Your Identity Is a Powerful Part of Your Story

I have had the privilege of serving as a pastor at the same church for more than thirty years. We teach a class at each of our campuses called *Intro to Faith*. It's a prerequisite for anyone desiring membership in our congregation, but more importantly, it provides a comfortable environment for people to pose any questions they have about the Bible, Christianity, or our church's beliefs.

To help our class members get to know one another better, we go around the first night and ask everyone to tell us their name and one important fact about themselves. I'm always fascinated by what people choose to say. Usually I hear several people talk about how recently they moved to town. Others share their occupation or champion their favorite sports team. I almost always have a few people tell me about their cats, and because it is our first night together, I do my best to smile and nod affirmatively.

One night, an eleven-year-old African-American girl walked in with two of her friends. Normally the class is for adults, but we make it clear that anyone is welcome. When this young girl's turn came to introduce herself, she unwaveringly said, "My name is Sharia, and Pastor Joey is teaching me to be a follower of Jesus."

I wish you could have observed the looks on the faces of everyone else in the class. This young girl's pointed answer melted our hearts. She fearlessly nailed it in a roomful of people far older than herself. In an economy of words, she gave us a powerful answer to the question, *Who are you?* Her response rolled off her lips so naturally and comfortably because that is the way she thinks about herself. She's learning to become a follower of Jesus, and that self-image impacts the way she chooses to view her life and the people around her. Even an eleven-year-old can choose to believe what God says about her.

You, too, have a running list of answers to that question playing in the background of your mind every day. *Who are you?*

It's there when you wake up in the morning. The answer is confirmed or challenged when you take your first look in the mirror. You carry your self-image around your house, your community, your workplace, and your church. That's one of the primary reasons you talk frequently, or do not talk at all. Your self-image goes a long way toward explaining why you are happy, or angry, or worried, or talkative, or shy, or hundreds of other behaviors and attitudes we could mention.

The plot thickens as you interact with the world around you. There's a steady stream of people, businesses, and institutions that want to tell you how to think about yourself. You need to be thinner. You're the most important person in the room. You're so beautiful. You need to work harder. You're dumb. You're a victim. You don't measure up. You deserve a new car. Often these analyses are filled with lies or half-truths that can impact your heart and life in all sorts of negative ways.

When was the last time you slowed down long enough to evaluate the way you've answered the question *Who are you?* Have you ever done that? What if you are carrying around an entire cluster of thoughts about yourself that are simply untrue? How damaging and demoralizing would that be? And how does your answer compare to what God says about *you?*

GOD'S WORD TO THE RESCUE

The Bible has an amazing number of ways to help you answer that question. Sometimes the Lord says it straight on with statements like, "You are _____." More often however, our heavenly Father gives metaphors or word pictures because he wants us to understand, remember, marvel over, and enjoy how our relationship with him impacts who we are.

The purpose of this book is to help you, or perhaps you and a select group of friends, to develop a biblical view of self. I hope to arm and challenge you with thirty-one crisp answers to help you think about yourself in a way that's consistent with what the God of heaven affirms to be true. Why thirty-one? I think it is helpful for us to set aside a full month to focus on this all-important aspect of our story. The chapters are purposely brief because I understand that we're all busy people.

I'm assuming you have already decided to become a follower of Jesus Christ. This material is written for those who are Christians. If that is not yet true of you, this book might be helpful as you contemplate the identity that is available to you in and through the shed blood of Jesus Christ. Welcome to the journey.

I also hope that as you read this book, you feel like you are having a comfortable conversation with someone who cares about your story. My training is in pastoral ministry and biblical counseling, and I have the privilege of spending hours each week talking to people. I have discovered over the years that the issue of self-image is a critical piece in the puzzle of growing closer to the Lord. It also impacts the way you relate to the people God has placed around you. Having a correct set of answers to the question *Who are you?* is vital to loving God and people well.

MEET OUR FELLOW TRAVELERS

I hope you don't mind, but I've invited a few others to join us in our conversation. Often it helps, when trying to practically apply a concept from God's Word, to think about how the principle would impact someone else's life. That's why the Bible is filled with narratives and stories. The Lord teaches us in living technicolor as we observe truths lived out in real-life examples in Scripture.

As we contemplate the Bible's various answers to our core question, we'll test-drive them in the stories of our newfound friends. Becoming skilled in the art of biblical application will serve you well on this journey.

First, please say hello to Andy. He's a hard-working employee at the local factory. His clothes are worn; his handshake is firm. But Andy struggles with anger—a lot. He often becomes sinfully angry at work, at home, at the ball field, and even at church. Andy carries a low-grade anger in his soul all day long. However, he carries something else— a running list of answers to the question *Who are you?* I wonder what those answers are. I wonder where they came from. I wonder if they are true. I wonder if they match what God would say.

Sitting next to Andy is Dee. She is a young Hispanic mother with two energy-filled children at home. Dee has gained weight since giving birth, and she doesn't like what she sees in the mirror. She is also tired all the time as she runs from changing diapers to making meals to satisfying her husband's seemingly unreasonable demands. Dee feels depressed, and though her doctor has prescribed an antidepressant for her, the feelings persist. Does the way Dee thinks about herself have any bearing on the way she feels? Does her heart have anything to do with her story?

Next comes Curt. Do you have any questions about what might be wrong in the world? Curt will happily tell you because he complains about everything. He can tell you about the shortcomings of the government. He can detail the failures of his wife, his children, his boss, his pastor, and the officers at the local police department. Generally, less than sixty seconds go by between the moment Curt opens his eyes in the morning and his first complaint comes spewing forth. In fact, Curt is a complaining machine. He has a well-defined way of thinking about himself. Not surprisingly, it's practically all jaded or downright incorrect.

Then there's Faye. Sweet Faye. She was trained in engineering and worked hard at a local company for forty years before retiring recently. Faye has a problem she rarely discusses with anyone. She is gripped with fear. Her engineering background has not prepared her for all the uncertainties that come at this stage of life. She cannot fix all her health problems. There's no spreadsheet capable of solving the tensions she has with her daughter-in-law, who refuses to let Faye see her grandchildren. Faye is afraid of the people who live in her deteriorating neighborhood and afraid of noises in the night. She barely recognizes the woman she sees in the mirror anymore. *Who am I?*, she asks. Good question. What would God say, and does Faye believe him?

Take a deep breath and say hello to Pete. What a piece of work. Pete is a college athlete who loves to talk about his accomplishments. His pride is thick and plentiful. He knows he's the most handsome person in the group, and the fastest, strongest, and the one with the most trophies on his living room mantle. If you don't know it yet, you will, because Pete loves to drone on about himself. However, he's terribly lonely because others do not seem nearly as interested in discussing Pete's wonderfulness as he does. There's not much doubt about what Pete thinks of himself. The question is, can he ever change?

Then there's Walt. You'll like Walt. He's a young African-American man who worked his way through college and just passed his CPA exam. Now he's an accountant at a solid firm and has a bright future. Three cheers for a fine young man like this. But wait a minute. Walt's heart is filled with worry. What if he can't measure up? What if he makes a mistake? What if he misses a house payment? What if his girlfriend is unfaithful? What if his company fails? His mind is crammed with worry. Who is Walt? What would Walt say? More importantly, what would Walt's God say?

There's one more chair in the circle. It's comfortable with soft leather and an ideal amount of padding. Amazingly, your favorite beverage is already on the adjoining table along with your Bible, a pen, and your well-worn notebook. Please have a seat because *you* have an important story as well. In fact, yours might help Walt, while Faye's might help yours. We might even find a way to help proud Pete, although have you noticed? He's getting on our nerves already.

You have an answer to the question *Who are you?* In fact, you have a lot of answers. The question we need to answer over the next thirty-one days is this: *How does God want your answers to change?* Let's get started on the task of aligning our self-image with God's sufficient and relevant Word.

CHAPTER 1

You Are Created

The Bible wastes no time answering the question before us. In an economy of words, God explains how he created the heavens and the earth. The descriptions are crisp and riveting:

- The earth was formless and void.

- Then God said, "Let there be light."

- Let the earth spout vegetation.

- Let the waters team with living creatures.

No wonder the psalmist would later proclaim, "The heavens are telling of the glory of God; and their expanse is declaring the work of his hands" (Psalm 19:1). Look to the sky on a starry night and contemplate the power and majesty of our creator God.

Then Genesis 1 makes a startling revelation—next, God created human beings. Imagine what that day would have been like.

> God said, "Let Us make man in Our image, according to Our likeness; and let them rule over the fish of the sea and over the birds of the sky and over the cattle and over all the earth, and over every creeping thing that creeps on the

earth." God created man in His own image, in the image of God He created him; male and female He created them (Genesis 1:26-27).

ARE YOU KIDDING ME?

The Lord has blessed my wife and me with four grandsons. Our three-year-old Jack (whom his parents have affectionately nicknamed Jacknado) and I love playing a game with one another while talking on FaceTime. I'll make a statement, and he'll say, "Are you kidding me, Papa?" Next, he'll make a statement, and I'll respond in kind. Then we break out in giggles as if we're the funniest people on earth.

Contemplating the implications of Genesis 1:26-27 is an "Are you kidding me?" moment for sure. However, the joy is not because of Grandpa's silliness—it's the delicious notion that an essential aspect of our identity is that we were purposely and personally created by God himself.

Walt, I wonder if that could impact the way you think about the situations that worry you? Pete, should this truth affect the way you talk about your accomplishments? Faye, if God created you, is he also powerful enough to provide help that will replace your fears with calm and confidence?

IN GOD'S IMAGE

In the ancient world, kings established images of themselves as a powerful reminder to everyone of their presence and position. Amazingly, the Lord created human beings to be visible representations of him. We were given a position of dominion over other aspects of creation so that we could joyfully serve and submit to our rightful king and, in so doing, give others a better understanding of his character.

Christ affirmed that truth in a marvelous sermon he preached on a mountainside: "Let your light shine before men in such a way that they may see your good works, and glorify your Father who is in heaven"

(Matthew 5:16). He did not say that to the rocks, or the trees, or the animals in the vicinity. He said it to human beings because we are uniquely created in his image.

David wrote a song about this astounding truth. This may have been written one night as he watched over his flock of sheep:

> When I consider Your heavens, the work of Your fingers, the moon and the stars, which You have ordained; what is man that You take thought of him, and the son of man that You care for him? Yet You have made him a little lower than God, and You crown him with glory and majesty! You make him to rule over the works of Your hands; You have put all things under his feet, all sheep and oxen, and also the beasts of the field, the birds of the heavens and the fish of the sea, whatever passes through the paths of the seas. O LORD, our Lord, how majestic is Your name in all the earth! (Psalm 8:3-9).

David was wise to contemplate these ideas. They helped him understand his position in God's plan. We have been crowned "with glory and majesty" because of the potential we have to represent our God well.

While our culture might think that Dee's care for her children is insignificant, the Bible tells a far different story of what her faithful and sacrificial love represents. When Walt performs his accounting tasks with integrity and truthfulness, he is giving others a right opinion of his God. Both Dee and Walt are living out the importance and dignity of their created purpose.

WE SHOULD PRAISE HIM

This truth should motivate us to thank and honor our God, who created us in this fashion. That even includes all our quirks and idiosyncrasies because the Lord knows about every one of them. In another Psalm, David explained:

> You formed my inward parts; You wove me in my
>   mother's womb.
> I will give thanks to You, for I am fearfully and
>   wonderfully made;
> Wonderful are Your works, and my soul knows it very
>   well.
> My frame was not hidden from You, when I was made in
>   secret,
> *and* skillfully wrought in the depths of the earth;
> Your eyes have seen my unformed substance; and in your
>   book were all written.
> The days that were ordained for me, when as yet there was
>   not one of them.
> How precious also are Your thoughts to me, O God!
>   How vast is the sum of them!
> If I should count them, they would outnumber the sand.
>   When I awake, I am still with You (Psalm 139:13-18).

David's response to these magnificent truths was to give thanks to God. Our position in the Lord's created order is because of his power, not ours. The result of reflecting on how God views us should be amazement, not pride. The fact that God formed us individually in our mother's womb and then gave us the possibility and responsibility to represent him on his earth is a jaw-dropping reality. The next time you look in the mirror, pause and consider this astounding reality: You are created by God.

WITH THE ABILITY TO WORSHIP

The Bible's final book echoes this same theme.

> Worthy are You, our Lord and our God, to receive glory and
> honor and power; for You created all things, and because of
> Your will they existed, and were created (Revelation 4:11).

> Every created thing which is in heaven and on the earth
> and under the earth and on the sea, and all things in them,

I heard saying, "To Him who sits on the throne, and to the Lamb, be blessing and honor and glory and dominion forever and ever" (Revelation 5:13).

Curt should think about this as he complains with the tongue God created. So should Andy as he recalls the many times he has exercised his God-given emotions by venting and exploding on the people around him. Is this why God created them? Are they worshipping their Creator with such words and actions? Remembering their identity calls them to something far better. Will they choose to believe what God says about them?

The good news is that God stands ready to help us change. He is remaking us in the image of his Son (Romans 8:28-29), the one who enables us to progressively live more consistently with the purpose for which we were made. Rejoice that an essential aspect of your identity is that you are created by the God of heaven and earth!

QUESTIONS FOR PERSONAL REFLECTION

1. How should the fact that you are created impact the way you think and live each day?

2. If this concept of being created by God had a more prominent place in your identity, what would be different in your life, your thinking, your relationships?

3. Which of the individuals in our study are most like you? Explain your answer.

QUESTIONS FOR GROUP DISCUSSION

Note: I have designed these questions so either individuals or groups can respond to them.

1. What are some of the characteristics of men and women who view themselves through the lens of being created in God's image?

2. Work together to find applications of this biblical truth of being created as it relates to Andy, Dee, Curt, Faye, Pete, and Walt. How should this truth affect their thoughts and desires? How should it affect their words and actions?

3. What are some ways this truth could impact you in a practical way? If you are in a group, consider asking for accountability as you move forward together.

CHAPTER 2

You Have a
God-Created Purpose

Recently, I had my annual eye exam with an ophthalmologist from our church. The doctors in our congregation watch over my health like hawks, and I'm appreciative of the high-quality care I receive. At the end of the exam, she updated the prescription for my glasses and recommended a store close to the urban community center where I work. I prefer shopping locally whenever possible, so on one of my lunch hours, I headed over to see what was available.

The array of choices was dizzying. Frames of every conceivable shape and texture. Lens colors that ran the entire spectrum of the rainbow. I also had to decide if I wanted bifocals, trifocals, or progressive lenses. As I tried on a number of options, I was amazed at how differently the world around me appeared. Some brought greater clarity while many others distorted what I saw. There was also the issue of what happened when I looked at myself in the mirror. Different styles not only changed the way the world looked—they changed the way I saw myself. One pair made me appear to be a rock star (kind of), another a computer geek, and still another a studious fellow. I will let you decide which option you think I chose.

The same is true of a Christian's purpose. Few aspects of a person's identity are more powerful and determinative than the goal you adopt each day and even each moment as you navigate the relationships and situations of everyday life. It's very much like waking up in the morning and sliding your glasses on your face. Your chosen purpose impacts the way you see the people and events around you. And, it impacts the way you see yourself as well.

Thankfully, the New Testament clearly explains God's purpose for us. Here are some of the seminal passages on this aspect of our identity:

> We know that God causes all things to work together for good to those who love God, to those who are called according to His purpose. For those whom He foreknew, He also predestined to become conformed to the image of His Son, so that He would be the firstborn among many brethren (Romans 8:28-29).

> We also have as our ambition, whether at home or absent, to be pleasing to Him (2 Corinthians 5:9).

> You did not choose Me but I chose you, and appointed you that you would go and bear fruit, and that your fruit would remain, so that whatever you ask of the Father in My name He may give to you (John 15:16).

There are many other places in Scripture that develop this theme in additional ways, but the core idea is the wonderful truth that God's purpose for his children is that we become more like Jesus Christ and more pleasing to him. This focus—when flowing out of a heart of adoration for the Lord and dependence on his strength—results in a kind of fruitfulness that is delightful and delicious to God and those around us.

AN AMAZING POSSIBILITY

Followers of Christ find this purpose to be an incredible reality. Christ is the One we adore, worship, and love. Even this morning, as my personal Bible reading took me to Mark 15–16, I was moved by the thought of Jesus' death, burial, and resurrection on my behalf. I have been a Christian for decades and I still find truths like these from the Word of God to be soothing and impactful. When you add the affirmation that I and my brothers and sisters in Christ can actually be changing and becoming more like Christ, this God-given purpose is a powerful and encouraging motivator. That's the pair of glasses I want to wear as often as possible.

The degree of your love for Christ will have a significant impact on your self-image. The more you adore him, the more you'll embrace the purpose of growing in his image. As you contemplate all the other goals and purposes you might adopt at any given moment, hopefully you will say with John the Baptist, "He must increase, but I must decrease" (John 3:30).

This is why a discussion on self-image is as much about Christology (the doctrine of Christ) as it is anthropology (the doctrine of humanity). Wise believers drink deeply from Christ-focused passages such as these:

> God, after He spoke long ago to the fathers in the prophets in many portions and in many ways, in these last days has spoken to us in His Son, whom He appointed heir of all things, through whom also He made the world. And He is the radiance of His glory and the exact representation of His nature, and upholds all things by the word of His power. When He had made purification of sins, he sat down at the right hand of the Majesty on high, having become as much better than the angels, as He has inherited a more excellent name than they (Hebrews 1:1-4).

> He is the image of the invisible God, the firstborn of all creation. For by Him all things were created, both in the heavens and on earth, visible and invisible, whether thrones or dominions or rulers or authorities—all things have been created through Him and for Him. He is before all things,

and in Him all things hold together. He is also head of the body, the church; and He is the beginning, the firstborn from the dead, so that He Himself will come to have first place in everything (Colossians 1:15-18).

...so that Christ may dwell in your hearts through faith; and that you, being rooted and grounded in love, may be able to comprehend with all the saints what is the breadth and length and height and depth, and to know the love of Christ which surpasses knowledge, that you may be filled up to all the fullness of God (Ephesians 3:17-19).

What pair of glasses should you choose each day as you think about your purpose? The ones that help you focus clearly on finding ways to become more like our wonderful Savior.

A PRACTICAL OUTLOOK

The small group we met in the introduction agrees that this aspect of our self-image has the potential to dramatically impact the choices we make in both the inner and outer person each day. Everyone notices that Andy's head is bowed and his mood is reflective. He asks out loud if this could have anything to do with the times he becomes sinfully angry. Sweet Faye says, "Andy, I love how transparent you are. Can you tell us about a recent time when you were angry?"

"It all seems so silly now," Andy says. He goes on to describe an event a few days ago when he blew up at his wife. He had worked hard all day and simply wanted to be shown a measure of thanks for his labors. On the way home, he even thought about how great it would be if his wife were waiting for him with a glass of iced tea and a word of appreciation.

That's not quite the way things unfolded. Instead, his wife had a bad day herself and was looking down at her smartphone when Andy came through the door. A few minutes later, she looked up and asked if he was going to cut the grass that night because it was looking straggly.

That was all it took. Andy flew into a profanity-laced rage about how she never gave him any thanks or respect. The kids ran for cover as they typically did when dad was coming unglued.

Andy looked at the group mournfully and said, "Sadly, Jesus was nowhere in the picture. I wasn't concerned about seeking his strength as I spent time with my family. I did not care about how a better response could have helped me become more like Christ, or to image Jesus to my family members in that moment. My purpose was being respected and appreciated—and by the time I pulled in the driveway, those goals had reached idol status in my heart."

The group didn't judge their hurting friend because they, too, had ready examples of how they had chosen to view themselves through a skewed pair of glasses instead of through the purpose God has given them. They walked back through Andy's incident together, this time thinking about what his desires, thoughts, words, and actions would have looked like had he believed what God's Word said about him. He asked his friends to hold him accountable for finding specific ways to make God's goal of his growing toward Christlikeness his goal as well.

QUESTIONS FOR PERSONAL REFLECTION

1. Who do you know that finds practical ways to accomplish God's purpose of growing toward Christlikeness? Describe the way that person lives and the impact it has on you.

2. How frequently do you choose to think about yourself through this all-important lens of growing toward Christlikeness?

3. What would be different in your life and relationships if becoming more like Christ was your foremost priority each day?

QUESTIONS FOR GROUP DISCUSSION

1. Role-play what Andy's incident could have been like if he had done a better job of thinking about himself through the lens of God's purpose for him. Start from the moment he left work and continue to the point where his wife made her remark about the lawn. In what ways could Andy have been more Christlike?

2. What are some examples of wrong goals that sometimes get in the way of becoming more like Christ?

3. Walk through what a typical day could and should be like if we were more diligent to think about ourselves in terms of growing more Christlike. What role does the gospel play in this process?

CHAPTER 3

You Are Fallen

The members of your small group are beginning to feel more comfortable with one another. Everyone has found it helpful and instructive to think about being created by God as his image-bearers and then given the incredible purpose and privilege of pleasing him and becoming more like his Son. As your group gathers again, several members are able to joyfully report specific opportunities over the previous week to apply their learning to situations they faced in real time.

Andy spoke about his newfound desire to drive home from work thinking about himself through the lens of the goal of pleasing God regardless of any shortcomings he perceived in the members of his family. Faye then turned to him and said, "Andy, every day this week I asked the Lord to give you the strength to do just that. I'm so glad he did."

Andy seemed genuinely moved by her words and went on to explain that while things did not go perfectly the past seven days, he was seeing changes in his interactions as he tried to adjust the way he thought about himself. "I really want to learn to believe what God says about me and act on it in real life."

Then Walt spoke. "I've been thinking a lot about why all of this is so hard. My goals are so often in conflict with what God desires."

Most everyone agreed they had a battle on their hands. Then Walt pulled out a book that his grandfather had just given him. "Grandpa was a pastor, so I asked him the other day why pleasing God was so difficult." The book his grandfather recommended to answer that question was *Not the Way It's Supposed to Be* by theologian Cornelius Plantinga. Walt asked if he could read a few lines, and everyone nodded in agreement.

> The awareness of sin used to be our shadow. Christians hated sin, feared it, fled from it, grieved over it. Some of our grandparents agonized over their sins. A man who lost his temper might wonder if he could still go to Holy Communion. A woman who for years envied her more attractive and intelligent sister might worry that this sin threatened her very salvation.[1]

"Wow," Pete exclaimed. "For a guy named Cornelius, he sounds like he might actually understand what's happening in our hearts and lives today. He's right. We don't talk about sin very often anymore." The members of the group looked at one another with a mixture of both fear and anticipation. Could the theologian recommended by Walt's grandpa be on to something?

AS FAR AS THE CURSE IS FOUND

After the creation narratives in Genesis 1–2, Scripture quickly explains how and why living in a way that is consistent with our God-given design is so elusive: *sin*. That little word has huge implications. To make the point obvious and the implications unmistakable, the Lord places his image-bearers in a perfect garden and gives them one simple command. You have heard the comment "You had only one job." Adam and Eve had only one command. But they also had a tempter, our adversary the devil, who suggested that God was not good and that living for the lust of the flesh, the lust of the eyes, and the pride of life (1 John 2:16) would bring greater joy and fulfillment. He even made a sinister promise about the rebellion they were contemplating: "You surely will not die!" (Genesis 3:4).

Our ancestors took the bait and plunged the entire human race into a constant battle with sin and death. Paul develops this theme in his epic description of human nature apart from Christ:

> Just as through one man sin entered into the world, and death through sin, and so death spread to all men, because all sinned—for until the Law sin was in the world, but sin is not imputed when there is no law. Nevertheless death reigned from Adam until Moses, even over those who had not sinned in the likeness of the offense of Adam, who is a type of Him who was to come (Romans 5:12-14).

Back in the garden, the trap was sprung, and the consequences of abandoning God's design and purpose began at a breathtaking pace. Satan promised Adam and Eve that their pride and rebellion would lead to greater life, but the opposite began happening immediately. Death in the Bible always involves separation, and when Adam and Eve chose to no longer believe what God had said about them, they began dying. For the first time in their existence, they were ashamed and hid themselves from their Creator because their relationship with him was dying. When God asked Adam what he had done, the first husband blamed his wife because their marriage was dying. The consequences for refusing to believe what God had said about them were bitter and disappointing.

In the subsequent chapters of Genesis, the next generation of image-bearers move so far away from their design and purpose that out of jealousy and anger, Cain rises up and murders his brother Abel. The shock of that event reverberates even to John's first epistle, where he says, "Not as Cain, who was of the evil one and slew his brother. And for what reason did he slay him? Because his deeds were evil" (1 John 3:12). That is what happens when we refuse to believe what God says about us. We choose purposes and identities that lead to a dizzying array of attitudes and actions that displease God and result in death on an amazing number of levels.

By the end of Genesis 4, one of Cain's descendants, Lamech, is not only killing someone, but writing a boastful song about what he has done and sharing it with his family. Next, we turn the page and read the first of many genealogies in the Bible. Each generation listed is a painful reminder of the extent of sin's curse: so-and-so was born and he lived a certain number of years and he died. And he died. And he died. The message comes screaming out to anyone with ears to hear: Choosing sinful goals and purposes over God's design and plan always leads to pain and death.

MUCH MORE THAN JUST BEHAVIOR

Any book about a Christian's identity, as stated in Scripture, must deal with the reality and implications of the fall. The good news of the gospel is best understood against the backdrop of the bad news of our sinful condition.

Careful students of God's Word know that the really bad news is that sin is not simply something we do with our hands. Rebellion and pride reside in the deepest recesses of our hearts. The prophet Jeremiah graphically explained, "The heart is more deceitful than all else and is desperately sick; who can understand it?" (Jeremiah 17:9).

According to the Bible, our hearts are far more than simply the seat of our emotions. The word *heart* is the most comprehensive word in Scripture to describe the inner person, the control center, who we really are at the very core of our being. It is the place where our beliefs, desires, emotions, and thoughts reside. The truth we have to face about our identities is that every aspect of our being has been tainted by sin. We are fallen creatures.

ABOUT THAT LOG

Facing this truth head-on is hard for God's image-bearers. We would prefer to blame our choices on our circumstances or the people around us. Too often we sound like Adam when he sheepishly pronounced, "The woman whom you gave to be with me, she gave me from the tree" (Genesis 3:12).

Perhaps this is why Jesus taught, in his first recorded sermon, that we fallen image-bearers must honestly face this truth:

> Why do you look at the speck that is in your brother's eye, but do not notice the log that is in your own eye? Or how can you say to your brother, "Let me take the speck out of your eye," and behold, the log is in your own eye? You hypocrite, first take the log out of your own eye, and then you will see clearly to take the speck out of your brother's eye (Matthew 7:3-5).

By God's grace, our fallen condition is not the end of the story—far from it. But it is an important aspect of our identity and we dare not ignore it.

A SOBERING REALITY

The group was quiet and reflective. Finally, Curt broke the silence. "Walt, I'm glad your grandfather gave you that book. This theologian is right—sin is the problem. I can't wait to get home and tell my wife and kids about this explanation for their failures. Then tomorrow at lunch, I'm going to talk to my co-workers. It's high time someone told them about their sin. This is what's wrong with politicians, and athletes, and professors and..." Suddenly Curt stopped mid-sentence. "Hey, wait a minute..."

Friends, I think we may have just had a breakthrough.

QUESTIONS FOR PERSONAL REFLECTION

1. When you think of sin, is it generally in reference to yourself or to someone else?

2. What role, if any, does the concept of sin have in the way you think about yourself? What role should it play?

3. Are you in the habit of asking for forgiveness from God and other people when you sin against them?

QUESTIONS FOR GROUP DISCUSSION

1. Read again the quote Walt read from *Not the Way It's Supposed to Be.* What is your response to these words? Why is the point made in these words so important to understand?

2. Describe the character and behavior of people who have learned to factor the reality of the fall (sin) into their daily living.

3. What do you think just occurred to Curt at the end of this chapter? What do you think he says next? What impact should his realization have upon us?

CHAPTER 4

You Are Loved

H ey, wait a minute," Curt exclaimed. "Can we replay that log and speck thing for a minute? Are you telling me I should look at the ways I displease God first before complaining about everyone and everything else? That would be a totally different way of thinking about myself."

"Dude," said Pete, "that would be a totally different way for any of us to think about ourselves." Everyone in the circle nodded in agreement.

Pete continued, "I wonder what makes living that way so hard?"

"I think I know, at least for me," said Dee. "I don't like to admit my failures because I think God is so disappointed with me already. Why make him any more disgusted?"

That thought hung in the air for several moments until Walt broke the silence. "Dee, your authenticity just reminded me about one of Grandpa's sermons about the prodigal son. Grandpa said we need to remember that when we admit our failures to God, he relates to us like a loving father."

"I don't think I've ever heard that story," Curt said. "Walt, would you tell it to us?"

A POWERFUL STORY

The parable of the prodigal son is recorded in Luke 15, toward the end of Jesus' public ministry. By this time he had been formally rejected by the religious leaders of the day, but curiously, many tax collectors and sinners are choosing to place their faith and trust in him. Luke explained the problem succinctly: "Both the Pharisees and the scribes began to grumble, saying, 'This man receives sinners and eats with them'" (Luke 15:2).

The reactions on each person's face revealed that everyone in the group was struck by that statement. It especially seemed to resonate with Dee, who looked at Walt more attentively.

As Jesus responded to the Pharisees and scribes, he began with two shorter parables—one about a lost sheep, and another about a lost coin. The stories emphasized the great lengths the respective owners went to find what had been lost, and the incredible joy they expressed when the items were found. Everyone nodded as they heard about the owners' responses:

> "Rejoice with me, for I have found my sheep which was lost!" (verse 6).

> "Rejoice with me, for I have found the coin which I had lost!" (verse 9).

Quietly, each person wondered, *Is that the way God feels about me?* Jesus answered that question clearly when he closed each of the first two stories with the same conclusion:

> I tell you that in the same way, there will be more joy in heaven over one sinner who repents than over ninety-nine righteous persons who need no repentance (verse 7).

> I tell you, there is joy in the presence of the angels of God over one sinner who repents (verse 10).

Curt was starting to connect the dots. "It's a lot easier to believe and affirm what God says about my sin if I know he still chooses to love me in spite of my failures." Then he made a stunning confession: "To tell the truth, I can't even remember the last time I admitted any sin to God or anyone else in my life. I'm not even sure how God would respond."

A LOST SON

Jesus, the master teacher, drew crowds everywhere he went. In Luke 15, we see that even tax collectors and sinners were coming to listen to him. Imagine their deep spiritual thirst as they came with the full knowledge that up till now, their life choices had left them empty, hopeless, and convinced that a holy God had no interest in them. The self-righteous Pharisees and scribes were there as well, grumbling in disdain as they saw the assembled crowd.

Jesus began his third parable, saying, "A man had two sons" (verse 11). The mention of two sons may have caught people's attention because in the first two parables, the focus was on one sheep and one coin.

The details unfolded in rapid-fire succession. The youngest son brazenly demanded his inheritance and then "went on a journey into a distant country, and there he squandered his estate with loose living" (verse 13).

Curt and Pete looked at each other. Both said, "I know what that's like." Andy nodded. "Yeah, and the guilt can be unreal."

The younger son's friends ran out as quickly as his money, and he was left impoverished. Destitute for food, this Jewish man suffered the indignity of working as a simple laborer feeding unclean swine.

"I bet the Pharisees and scribes smiled at that part," Faye said.

"He got exactly what he deserved," said Dee. "I imagine his father was upset and disappointed. I know that's the way God thinks about me. I think of this story every time I look in the mirror."

"So what did this rebel do next?" asked Pete. "It sounds like he had a massive log in his eye."

A COURAGEOUS CHANGE

Thankfully, the son "came to his senses" (verse 17). In a moving example of repentance, he began to think about himself correctly:

> When he came to his senses, he said, "How many of my father's hired men have more than enough bread, but I am

dying here with hunger! I will get up and go to my father, and will say to him, 'Father, I have sinned against heaven, and in your sight; I am no longer worthy to be called your son; make me as one of your hired men'" (verses 17-19).

"Wow," said Curt. "It sounds like he is believing what God would say about him. He's finally focusing on the log in his eye first. Too bad he blew it so badly with his father."

A LOVING FATHER

"So let's hear the rest, Walt. The father disowned him, didn't he?" one group member asked.

Walt smiled, just like he had seen his Grandpa do from the pulpit so many times before. "No, my friends, that is not even close to what happened."

He got up and came to his father. But while he was still a long way off, his father saw him and felt compassion for him, and ran and embraced him and kissed him. And the son said to him, "Father, I have sinned against heaven and in your sight; I am no longer worthy to be called your son." But the father said to his slaves, "Quickly bring out the best robe and put it on him, and put a ring on his hand and sandals on his feet; and bring the fattened calf, kill it, and let us eat and celebrate; for this son of mine was dead and has come to life again; he was lost and has been found." And they began to celebrate (verses 20-24).

Walt then explained that there was more to the story. Sadly, the older brother was not nearly as forgiving, just like the Pharisees and scribes. But for the group's purposes that day, the key was understanding that they could believe what God said about their sin because he would respond to their repentant heart like a loving father, ready to lavish them with forgiveness and grace.

A PARADIGM SHIFT

Everyone in the circle sat quietly, somewhat stunned, as if they had just seen a final scene in a movie take an entirely unexpected twist. Then Dee cried softly. Faye moved over to comfort her, which made the tears come more profusely.

"God isn't disgusted with me when I'm an imperfect mom," Dee whispered to no one in particular. "He's not quick to judge when I fail as a wife. He doesn't hate me because I've put on weight. He's like the loving father in this story, isn't he?"

This realization hit hard for everyone in the group. Finally, Curt said, "I'm ready to be much more honest about the logs in my eye because this is the way God responds when I admit my wrongdoing. I want to believe what he says about me."

QUESTIONS FOR PERSONAL REFLECTION

1. How open are you about your fallenness? Do you find yourself confessing your sins regularly to God and others?

2. How does your view of God impact your willingness to face the areas of sin in your life?

3. Do you allow God's unfailing love for you to motivate you toward growth and change? How could the Father's unfailing love impact you and your sense of self?

QUESTIONS FOR GROUP DISCUSSION

1. How might the truth of God's love impact each of the group members in practical ways?

2. Why is it so easy to be like Dee and doubt the Father's love? Describe what that tendency looks like in real life.

3. How should the truth of God's love impact you, as well as anyone in your group?

CHAPTER 5

You Are Redeemed

The group wasn't even seated before Curt blurted out, "You guys won't believe what happened this week. My wife, Carla, almost fainted—I thought we were going to have to call 9-1-1!"

"Oh, no," said Dee. "Was it serious? I hope she's going to be all right."

"Maybe that wasn't the best choice of words," Curt said. "I mean, I decided to try something this week that shocked her."

"Wow, this sounds exciting," said Pete. "Do you want to tell us about it?"

"I thought a lot this week about the story of the prodigal son," Curt responded. "I couldn't get that parable out of my mind."

"Me neither," Andy said. "Maybe that's why they say the Bible is sharper than any two-edged sword. The Holy Spirit can use it to convict our hearts."

"No doubt about that," Curt said. "I just kept thinking, *I'm that guy.* I've squandered so many relationships by being such a critical person. But if God would respond to my admission with love and forgiveness, what am I waiting for?"

"So what did you do next?" Faye asked.

"I spent some time out on my deck one evening just talking to God about all of it. I did what the prodigal son did: I asked God to forgive me. I asked him to help me be more encouraging and thankful and less critical. The peace that came over me was amazing. I usually leave conversations more anxious because all I've done is criticize everyone else. When I admitted my sin, I sensed God's love and forgiveness immediately—just as happened with the father and his prodigal son."

"This is amazing," Pete said. "Then what?"

"Well," Curt continued, "the person I'm most critical of is Carla, so I decided I needed to ask her forgiveness. It was like, if God loves me when I'm honest about who I am, what do I have to lose?

"So I found Carla in the living room and asked if we could talk," Curt said. "She was apprehensive at first, probably because she knows that usually when I want to talk, it's to tell her something else I don't like about her. I explained what we've been studying in our group, and I confessed I had been sinning against her and a lot of other people with my speech. I asked her to forgive me, and I told her you guys would hold me accountable to change."

"What did she say?" Dee asked.

"She didn't seem to know what to say," Curt said. "At first she thought I was joking around. She even asked if an alien had invaded my body. But she finally said she would forgive me. Then she said what she really wanted to see was lasting change. And based on her history with me, I don't blame her one bit for being skeptical."

"So how do you feel about all of this now?" Faye asked.

"I'm more convinced of God's love for me than ever," Curt said. "Walt, I'm so glad you told us that story last week. But as I think about the ways I've used my tongue all these years, I feel like I am buried under this huge pile of sin."

Is Curt right about that?

THE ANTICIPATION OF REDEMPTION

Curt, like the rest of us, has to decide whether he will believe what God says about his past sins. He has already taken important steps forward. He repented—that is, he turned his heart and mind around and began to view his critical speech in an entirely different way. Believing that God was a loving heavenly Father motivated Curt to ask forgiveness of both the Lord and his wife, Carla. Now he needs to believe what God's Word says about redemption.

Feel free to cue the Christmas music, because while we could discuss this great truth from many different biblical perspectives, one of the most delightful occurs in a series of Scripture passages we often consider around Christmastime. When Mary and Joseph brought baby Jesus to the temple, they met two amazing people: Simeon and Anna.

Anna was an eighty-four-year-old widow who "never left the temple, serving night and day with fastings and prayers" (Luke 2:37). She thanked God upon seeing Jesus. When Simeon saw Joseph and Mary with Jesus, he took the child into his arms and made this shocking statement:

> Now Lord, You are releasing Your bond-servant to depart in peace, according to Your word; for my eyes have seen Your salvation, which You have prepared in the presence of all peoples, a Light of revelation to the Gentiles, and the glory of Your people Israel (Luke 2:29-32).

Mary and Joseph must have been reeling from that amazing pronouncement. Luke reports Anna's response as well: "At that very moment she came up and began giving thanks to God, and continued to speak of Him to all those who were looking for the redemption of Jerusalem" (verse 38).

"The *redemption* of Jerusalem" is a fascinating word choice. Luke reported earlier in his Gospel that when Mary visited her cousin Elizabeth, the mother of John the Baptist, she affirmed that her spirit had "rejoiced in God my Savior" (Luke 1:47). Zacharias, John the Baptist's father, rejoiced because the Lord God of Israel had "visited us and accomplished redemption for his people, and...raised up a horn of salvation for us" (Luke 1:68-69). When Jesus was born, the angel told the shepherds that "today in the city of David there has been born for you a Savior, who is Christ the Lord" (Luke 2:11). Now this picture of redemption is completed as Anna rejoices because this divine infant is the answer for "all those who were looking for the redemption of Jerusalem" (verse 38).

THE CENTRALITY OF REDEMPTION

The word *redemption* means "buy back." A price is paid to acquire something of value. In Christian theology, redemption describes the process of Jesus dying to pay for the sins of those who choose to believe in him. We are then released from the penalty, the power—and ultimately, in heaven—the presence of our sin. "Jesus paid it all," as the old hymn goes. This gets to the very core of what it means to believe what God says about us.

The importance of this concept is demonstrated by its inclusion in what some Bible students consider the heart of the Bible:

> All have sinned and fall short of the glory of God, being justified as a gift by His grace through the redemption which is in Christ Jesus; whom God displayed publicly as a propitiation in His blood through faith. This was to demonstrate His righteousness, because in the forbearance of God He passed over the sins previously committed; for the demonstration, I say, of His righteousness at the present time, so that He would be just and the justifier of the one who has faith in Jesus (Romans 3:23-26).

Going back to Curt's question about being buried in a pile of sins, the answer is that by God's grace, those sins have been paid for through the precious blood of Christ. Curt now needs to believe what God says about him: "As far as the east is from the west, so far has He removed our transgressions from us" (Psalms 103:12).

THE PURPOSE OF REDEMPTION

Paul also explained the intended effect of redemption to the churches in Ephesus:

...to the praise of the glory of His grace, which He freely bestowed on us in the Beloved. In Him we have redemption through His blood, the forgiveness of our trespasses, according to the riches of His grace which He lavished on us (Ephesians 1:6-8).

In Him, you also, after listening to the message of truth, the gospel of your salvation—having also believed, you were sealed in Him with the Holy Spirit of promise, who is given as a pledge of our inheritance, with a view to the redemption of God's own possession, to the praise of His glory (verses 13-14).

Everyone in the group nodded and expressed their thankfulness for their discussion. Dee shared, "I want everyone to know that I really appreciate each of you. These conversations are changing the way I think about myself. And Curt, I am so thankful for your transparency. You are not the only one who tends to think about himself as being buried under a pile of sins. Starting today, I'm going to try to believe what God says about me. Those sins have been cast as far as the east is from the west because of my Savior's precious blood. Imagine it—I am redeemed!"

QUESTIONS FOR PERSONAL REFLECTION

1. Do you tend to view yourself as being buried under a pile of sins? How does this affect you?

2. What practical steps could you take to make the truth about your redemption a more prominent part of your thinking?

3. What is the relationship between believing what God says about your redemption, and developing a willingness to confess sin?

QUESTIONS FOR GROUP DISCUSSION

1. How can each person in the group—Andy, Curt, Dee, Walt, Faye, and Pete—benefit from meditating on how the doctrine of redemption applies to them?

2. How can Curt's redemption sustain him even if Carla is slow to forgive him?

3. What impact can the doctrine of redemption have on the way Curt responds to future temptations to be critical of others?

CHAPTER 6

You Are Adopted

The Viars family has been assembled in a rather unconventional manner. Each of our children have different biological fathers and mothers. After my wife, Kris, and I conceived our first daughter Bethany naturally, we were unable to have additional children.

Our hearts would break each evening as we would hear little Bethany pray and ask God for a baby sister. She was far too young to understand an explanation of the biological issues involved, and we did not want to quench her childlike faith. But we saw no way Bethany would ever have a sister.

That was, until we received a call in the middle of the night from a local physician when Bethany was five. He was on the OB ward when a fellow doctor told him about a young unmarried couple who had just delivered a baby but wished to place the child for adoption. The baby was born prematurely, and the young couple had not yet formulated a plan for her care. The question to us that night essentially was, "Would you like a baby daughter?" Yes, we would eventually have to work through the formal legal process, but this newborn needed a safe home right away. I am somewhat hesitant to tell this story because I realize some families wait years to receive a call like that. But that is what happened.

We immediately woke Bethany, prayed about the decision, and had a middle-of-the-night worship service for God's incredible provision. We named our new daughter Karis, the New Testament Greek word that means "grace." To be able to adopt a child into our home was one of the greatest blessings we have ever received.

However, the Lord was not done. Two years later, we were contacted by a single expectant mother who asked if we would consider adopting her child. When Andrew was born, doctors determined that he was blind and had a cluster of special needs that would require life-long care. So we had the privilege of pursuing the adoption of another bundle of blessing into our home.

Andrew (aka "the Bear") is now twenty-nine years old. Kris has done a marvelous job of caring for him, and his sisters embraced the adventure with passion and creativity. Bethany and Karis are now married with two sons each, so our entire family has the joy of experiencing the power and pleasure of adoption firsthand.

One night, the Bear and I were out on a bike ride together. We have a recumbent tandem bike that sits low to the ground so Bear does not have to worry about falling. It has independent pedals and gears so we each get a good workout, and in God's sovereign plan (this may be a bit of a stretch), there's a frozen custard stand three miles from our house. We make that trip so frequently that when the Bear approaches the window to place our order, the young ladies behind the window just say, "Would you like the usual?" Bear thinks that is hilarious; we are treated as if we are movie stars or something.

On the way back, I was telling Bear something that I truly believe. Our lives would be far less enjoyable if the Lord had not allowed us to adopt him. Our family is much richer because of him and Karis. We love the privilege of adoption.

YOU ARE IN THAT SAME POSITION

What we studied back in chapter 3 was hard to face. We are fallen and cursed by sin. But as Paul reminded his readers in Rome, "Where sin increased, grace abounded all the more" (Romans 5:20). Because of the work of Christ on the cross, people like you and me can be adopted into the family of God. John emphasized this in the first chapter of his magnificent Gospel:

> As many as received Him, to them He gave the right to become children of God, even to those who believe in His name, who were born, not of blood nor of the will of the flesh nor of the will of man, but of God (John 1:12-13).

Please think carefully about the last phrase of that passage. God wanted to adopt *you*. He wanted *you* to be part of his family. And he did everything, including the sacrifice of his own Son, to make that a reality.

Our small-group friend Dee needs to remember that truth when she looks in the mirror. The most important thing about her is not that she gained some weight after giving birth or has a husband who is often dissatisfied. Instead, the essence of her identity is that she has been adopted into the family of God. Body image does not change that. Criticism from others does not change that. Just like our family was overjoyed when we were able to adopt our children, the Lord of heaven is overjoyed that Dee is one of his daughters.

YOU CAN OVERCOME YOUR FEAR OF FAILURE

Paul emphasized this theme in Romans 8. After an extended discussion about how the gospel empowers followers of Christ to grow in practical holiness in Romans 6–7, Paul told his brothers and sisters in Rome that the Holy Spirit, who lives inside us, secures our victory: "If the Spirit of Him who raised Jesus from the dead dwells in you, He who raised Christ Jesus from the dead will also give life to your mortal bodies through His Spirit who dwells in you" (Romans 8:11). We would all do well to ask ourselves if we really believe this is true of us.

Paul then tied this amazing truth to our adoption:

> You have not received a spirit of slavery leading to fear again, but you have received a spirit of adoption as sons by which

we cry out, "Abba! Father!" The Spirit Himself testifies with
our spirit that we are children of God, and if children, heirs
also, heirs of God and fellow heirs with Christ, if indeed
we suffer with Him so that we may also be glorified with
Him. For I consider that the sufferings of this present time
are not worthy to be compared with the glory that is to be
revealed to us (verses 15-18).

Because we have been adopted into the family of God, we do not
have to fear enslavement to sins of the past. When we struggle, we can
cry out "Abba! Father!" God is not aloof or distant. He loves us with
the intimate delight of a papa.

As a pastor, I've had the privilege of watching many godly parents
seeking to raise their children in the nurture and admonition of the
Lord. I love watching children who are especially thankful for a dad
who loves the Lord and loves them. The look on their faces says it all:
"This is my dad. I love him, and I'm glad to be in his family." That is
the happy position of every follower of Christ because we have been
adopted by our heavenly Father.

Our adoption also fortifies us for the suffering of this sin-cursed
world because we have eternal hope in Christ. "I consider that the sufferings of this present time are not worthy to be compared with the
glory that is to be revealed in us" (verse 18). Paul said that he "consid-
ers" this to be true of himself. He chose to believe what God has said
about him. So should we.

YOU CAN HAVE HOPE FOR THE FUTURE

Paul also emphasized this principle in Ephesians 1. He wrote,
"[God] predestined us to adoption as sons through Jesus Christ to Himself, according to the kind intention of His will, to the praise of the
glory of His grace, which He freely bestowed on us in the Beloved"
(verses 5-6).

Please note how the theme of God's will and sovereign grace runs through each of those passages. Our adoption was not an afterthought. It was part of God's eternal plan. He bestowed his grace on us freely in the beloved. That was the kind intention of his will. Choosing to believe this motivates us to live to the praise and glory of his grace.

QUESTIONS FOR PERSONAL REFLECTION

1. How has your adoption impacted the way you think about yourself? How should it?

2. What wrong evaluations of self could be replaced by this powerful truth from God's Word?

3. What does it mean for followers of Christ to live "to the praise of the glory of His grace"?

QUESTIONS FOR GROUP DISCUSSION

1. Take a moment to reflect on this aspect of the kind intention of God's will. How can this impact our response to suffering? If you're answering this as part of a group, have everyone take a turn at answering this.

2. What are some practical applications of this biblical truth to Andy, Dee, Curt, Faye, Pete, and Walt?

3. Describe followers of Christ who are choosing to believe this aspect of their identity. How do they think? What do they want? How do they feel? What do they say and do?

CHAPTER 7

You Are Forgiven

Recently I was counseling a couple from our community about some challenges they were facing in their marriage. Over the course of several sessions together, we studied what God's Word says about handling conflict by admitting sin and then both requesting and granting forgiveness. During this specific session, they told me about a disagreement they had the previous week, in which words were said on both sides that did not please God.

However, thankfully, later that day they met together and communicated in a godlier fashion. They admitted the ways they had sinned against the Lord and one another. Then they each sought the other's forgiveness, and in turn granted the same.

I was glad for what I was hearing and believed this was clear evidence of Jesus working in and through them. But I was unprepared for what transpired next. The wife looked at me and said, "But I'm still so ashamed of what I did."

THIS RAISES IMPORTANT QUESTIONS

Does the Lord want his children to live in shame even after they have admitted sin and requested and received forgiveness? Should guilt be a Christian's constant companion? Is that the way God wants us to think and live?

Choosing to believe what God's Word says about your forgiveness is an important part of your identity. John explained this principle in one of the first verses many followers of Christ commit to memory: "If we confess our sins, He is faithful and righteous to forgive us our sins and to cleanse us from all unrighteousness" (1 John 1:9). Two verses earlier, John explained the basis of this forgiveness: "the blood of Jesus His Son cleanses us from all sin" (verse 7).

Over the years, people have said to me, "But I don't feel forgiven." That brings us to one of the central aims of this book—to encourage and challenge you to choose to believe what God says about you even when your feelings may be raging in all sorts of directions.

A related objection is "But I just can't forgive myself." We are never commanded in Scripture to do such a thing. Instead, we are called to rejoice in Christ's finished work on the cross and the forgiveness we enjoy in him. This is why John reminds us that God is faithful and righteous to forgive. That is a foundation upon which you can rely. Please allow these words to be permanently impressed upon your mind. As a believer in Jesus, *you are forgiven*. God says so.

WHAT EXACTLY DOES FORGIVENESS ACCOMPLISH?

When God forgives our sins, does that mean he forgets them? Hardly. God is omniscient, which means he is all-knowing. However, forgiveness is much more powerful than passively forgetting. God actively chooses not to remember our sins as he determines how to deal with us today. That is the point of Psalm 103:12: "As far as the east is from the west, so far has he removed our transgressions from us."

The writer of Hebrews picks up this theme in Hebrews 10 as he discusses the superiority of the sacrifice of Jesus Christ, our high priest who shed his own blood for us.

> Every priest stands daily ministering and offering time after
> time the same sacrifices, which can never take away sins; but

He, having offered one sacrifice for sins for all time, sat down at the right hand of God, waiting from that time onward until His enemies be made a footstool for His feet. For by one offering He has perfected for all time those who are sanctified. And the Holy Spirit also testifies to us; for after saying, "This is the covenant that I will make with them after those days, says the Lord: I will put My laws upon their heart, and on their mind I will write them," He then says, "And their sins and their lawless deeds I will remember no more." Now where there is forgiveness of these things, there is no longer any offering for sin (verses 11-18).

This promise should amaze us. Because Jesus offered the perfect sacrifice, our heavenly Father will not remember our sins and lawless deeds. This is why our God does not want us to live in shame and guilt in response to all our failures and shortcomings. There is a much grander reality that should occupy our hearts and minds: the forgiveness we have received in Christ.

LET THE GOSPEL RESTORE YOUR JOY

David illustrates this process of repentance and forgiveness in Psalm 51 after repenting of his grievous sin with Bathsheba. He wrote:

Be gracious to me, O God, according to Your loving-kindness; according to the greatness of Your compassion blot out my transgressions. Wash me thoroughly from my iniquity and cleanse me from my sin. For I know my transgressions, and my sin is ever before me. Against You, You only, I have sinned and done what is evil in Your sight, so that You are justified when You speak and blameless when You judge (verses 1-4).

This act of repentance leads to a desire for forgiveness. "Purify me with hyssop, and I shall be clean; wash me, and I shall be whiter than snow. Make me to hear joy and gladness, let the bones which You have broken rejoice" (verses 7-8).

The effect of this supernatural cleansing is great joy in David's heart. "Restore to me the joy of Your salvation and sustain me with a willing spirit" (verse 12). Our guilt and shame are replaced with the delight of believing what God says about our sin.

MODEL YOUR FORGIVENESS OF OTHERS ON GOD'S FORGIVENESS OF YOU

There are many benefits to choosing to believe this truth. One is that you are better positioned to forgive those the Lord has placed around you. Paul made this point to the Christians in both Colossae and Ephesus:

> Bearing with one another, and forgiving each other, whoever has a complaint against anyone; just as the Lord forgave you, so also should you (Colossians 3:13).

> Be kind to one another, tender-hearted, forgiving each other, just as God in Christ also has forgiven you (Ephesians 4:32).

The more you bask in the way God has forgiven you, the better prepared you are to offer that same grace to others.

THE IMPLICATIONS ARE ENORMOUS

Each person in the group is becoming more comfortable with sharing how their discussions are impacting them at the heart level. They've developed a delightful trust in each other coupled with an increasing ability to apply biblical principles practically to their daily choices in life.

Pete spoke first. "I'm starting to realize that I have allowed my mind and speech to be very undisciplined. The reason I rarely think about the way God has forgiven me is because I'm too consumed with thoughts about my accomplishments. I guess that's why I end up bragging so much. I bet I have been pretty irritating to everyone in this circle."

Cue the awkward silence. By now everyone is beyond lying to one another or simply offering pious platitudes. Finally, Walt spoke. "Maybe so, Pete, but what you just admitted is really convicting to me too."

"Walt," Faye interjected, "I have never heard you brag about yourself."

"That is not what I meant," Walt said. "But I do let the worries of the day crowd out the joy I could have if I put more focus on the ways God has forgiven me. My heart needs to be more about God's gracious forgiveness and less about how I might make a mistake at work. What really bothers me about this is that I could have learned this lesson years ago, from Grandpa."

"What do you mean, Walt?" the others asked.

"Grandpa was a young black pastor in the 1960s. He experienced racial injustice in ways that are sad to contemplate. Yet somehow he still was a dignified and even joyful man. Church on Sundays was filled not just with honest lament but also exuberant praise. I asked Grandpa once how he dealt with the pain and anger of the way he and the members of his congregation had been treated. What you just said, Pete, reminded me of Grandpa's answer."

Walt continued. "Grandpa told me, 'There is more to my story than the ways others are mistreating me. I have been washed in the blood of the Lamb. This world is not my home because I am a forgiven man. I take great joy and delight in that.'"

Walt paused, then said, "By the way, I told Grandpa about our group, and he wants you to know that he is praying for us."

That made every face in the circle light up. "Walt, do you think your Grandpa would ever visit our group?" Dee asked. "I would love to hear more of his story, and to learn about his church. And, I would love to hear him pray."

Hmmm. Dee may be on to something here.

QUESTIONS FOR PERSONAL REFLECTION

1. Are shame and guilt ever your companions? What does this look like for you on a day-to-day basis?

2. What practical steps could you take to make God's forgiveness a more central aspect of your thinking?

3. What changes would take place in your life if your forgiveness in Christ was a more prominent part of your thinking each day?

QUESTIONS FOR GROUP DISCUSSION

1. As odd as it might seem initially, how are Pete and Walt similar?

2. Discuss the ways guilt and shame crop up in your thoughts and actions.

3. How does celebrating our forgiveness prepare us to handle the challenges of everyday living?

CHAPTER 8

You Are United with Christ

After the group was seated, Pete looked at Andy and said, "Andy, you asked us several weeks ago to hold you accountable for your anger at work. How's that going?" At an earlier stage in the group's relationship this question might have seemed inappropriate, but by now a level of transparency had developed to the point that everyone understood their important role of helping each other to become more like Christ.

Andy responded, "Thanks for asking me about that, Pete. I need my friends to keep checking in with me." The others nodded, affirming that they, too, wanted and needed such help themselves. Then Andy said a bit sheepishly, "I wasn't going to say anything about this because I didn't want to sound like I was bragging."

"But Andy, Pete asked you," Dee said. "We really want to know."

"Well, a guy came up to me at work the other day and asked what had happened to me. When I asked him what he meant, he told me I was not nearly as angry as I used to be. He even mentioned a couple of recent examples where my responses were totally different than before."

"That's so cool," Curt said. "What did you tell him?"

"Something I have never done before," Andy replied. "I told him I was a Christian and that I had been asking Jesus to help me handle my anger in a way that honored him."

THE SIGNIFICANCE OF OUR UNION

Andy is beginning to believe something very important about himself. In his earlier conversations, he acknowledged that when he began feeling angry, "Jesus was nowhere in the picture." But now he's consciously choosing to believe what God says about his unity with Christ. The New Testament is filled with passages in which followers of Jesus are said to be "in Christ" or "in him." Here are a few examples:

- "By His doing you are *in Christ Jesus*, who became to us wisdom from God, and righteousness and sanctification, and redemption" (1 Corinthians 1:30).

- "If anyone is *in Christ*, he is a new creature; the old things passed away; behold, new things have come" (2 Corinthians 5:17).

- "There is neither Jew nor Greek, there is neither slave nor free man, there is neither male nor female; for you are all *one in Christ Jesus*" (Galatians 3:28).

- "We are His workmanship, *created in Christ Jesus* for good works, which God prepared beforehand so that we would walk in them" (Ephesians 2:10).

- "We proclaim Him, admonishing every man and teaching every man with all wisdom, so that we may present every man *complete in Christ*" (Colossians 1:28).

- "The Lord Himself will descend from heaven with a shout, with the voice of the archangel and with the trumpet of God, and the *dead in Christ* will rise first" (1 Thessalonians 4:16).

Faye had a big smile on her face as she celebrated this victory with her friend. "This is amazing," she exclaimed. "Our pastor has been doing a series at church on this very topic. He has been encouraging us to preach the gospel to ourselves."

"What does he mean by that?" Pete asked.

"He said we should remind ourselves each day that when we trusted Christ as Savior and Lord, we were united with him in his death, burial, and resurrection," Faye said. "That is how Andy has been addressing his anger, and how he chose to respond when his co-worker noticed a difference. He could have just tried to change through human effort alone or accepted the compliment as if he were the one who made the difference. Andy has gone from 'Jesus is nowhere to be found' to 'I am united with Christ in everything I think, do, and say.'"

"Hmmm," Pete responded. "That is a great observation."

YOU HAVE DIED WITH CHRIST

Romans 6 is one of the clearest passages in the New Testament on our union with Christ. After writing five chapters that explain the sinfulness of humanity and the corresponding righteousness of God that can be credited to our accounts because of the work of Christ on the cross, Paul then focuses in Romans 6–8 on the practical implications of the gospel in everyday life. He explains our union with Jesus' death repeatedly in Romans 6:

- "Or do you not know that all of us who have been baptized into Christ Jesus have been baptized into His death?" (verse 3).

- "We have been buried with Him through baptism into death" (verse 4).

- "If we have become united with Him in the likeness of his death…" (verse 5).

- "Now if we have died with Christ…" (verse 8).

The implication of this truth is stunning. Paul raised this point because of the objection he anticipated to his teaching in Romans 1–5 that salvation was by grace alone, through faith alone, in Christ alone (see Romans 3:23-26). His detractors might have argued that this approach to salvation would result in lawless living. Paul explained that the opposite was true. When a person embraces the gospel, they are immediately united with Christ in his death. One of the most significant results is that the Christian is then freed from the power of sin. That is Paul's central point in Romans 6:6-7: "Knowing this, that our old self was crucified with Him, in order that our body of sin might be done away with, so that we would no longer be slaves to sin; for he who has died is freed from sin."

This is an important part of what it means to preach the gospel to yourself. You are choosing to believe what God has said about the fact you are no longer enslaved to sin. That is why one critical imperative in the passage instructs us to "consider yourselves to be dead to sin" (Romans 6:11).

YOU ARE UNITED WITH CHRIST'S RESURRECTION

What we have discussed so far is only the beginning of the good news. In Romans 6, Paul equally emphasizes how followers of Jesus are also united with Christ in his resurrection:

- "…so that as Christ was raised from the dead through the glory of the Father, so we too might walk in newness of life" (verse 4).

- "…certainly we shall also be in the likeness of his resurrection" (verse 5).

- "…we believe that we shall also live with Him" (verse 8).

This, too, is a truth Paul said we should learn to regularly factor into the way we think about ourselves. "Even so consider yourselves to be dead to sin, but alive to God in Christ Jesus" (verse 11). This gives God's children an entirely different motivation for and level of confidence in taking steps to become more like Jesus Christ.

HOW ABOUT YOU?

Up to now, we have periodically thought about how these truths can affect the various members of our counseling group. How are things going in *your* chair? Are you looking for specific ways to choose to believe what God says about you? Are you thinking more biblically about yourself? Pause and ask the Lord to help you experience breakthroughs similar to the one Andy enjoyed.

QUESTIONS FOR PERSONAL REFLECTION

1. How often do you think about your union with Christ?
   How is this chapter motivating you to focus more on this
   truth?

2. Read Romans 6:1-23 slowly and carefully. Do you have
   a working understanding of what this important chapter is all about? How would you briefly summarize your
   understanding?

3. What specific steps could you take to factor your union with
   Christ into the way you think about yourself every day?

QUESTIONS FOR GROUP DISCUSSION

1. Do you really believe it is possible for people like Andy to
   change the way this chapter describes?

2. Why is the doctrine of our union with Christ such a blessed
   and comprehensive truth for the believer?

3. How should this doctrine impact the way a Christian faces
   criticism? Or commendation? Or doubt? Or fear?

CHAPTER 9

You Are Righteous

My wife, Kris, and I have the privilege of entertaining hundreds of people in our home each year. Kris has developed several signature desserts, including one of my personal favorites, ice cream pie. She starts with a crushed graham-cracker crust, which is always a crowd favorite. Next comes a layer of hot fudge sauce (did I mention that I have a sweet tooth?). Then she places a generous layer of ice cream on top of the fudge sauce. We have learned that practically any flavor works, but coffee or mint chocolate chip are two of my favorites. Next comes more fudge sauce. On top of that comes whipped cream, sprinkles, and of course, a final drizzle of fudge sauce. Even the mere act of writing about this makes me wish we were entertaining a group tonight.

There is a sense in which what we have been studying so far in this book is like eating ice cream pie. Our identity in Christ is a combination of delicious truths that form an incredibly sweet way of thinking about oneself.

One of the reasons I love eating ice cream pie is that occasionally you hit an especially thick vein of fudge sauce. That is where our study of what God wants us to believe about ourselves brings us. While we have discussed amazing truths in each of the previous chapters, we now come to a concept that is almost too great to believe. In Christ, you are righteous.

Please pause and savor the richness of that spiritual truth. *Who are you?* According to the Bible, God has declared you to be righteous in him.

THE GREAT DILEMMA

Jesus explained in the Sermon on the Mount that "you are to be perfect, as your heavenly Father is perfect" (Matthew 5:48). On the one hand, that should not surprise us when we contemplate the holiness of God. The prophet Habakkuk was right when he said of our Lord, "Your eyes are too pure to approve evil, and You cannot look on wickedness with favor" (Habakkuk 1:13).

On the other hand, we know that we fall far short of this standard of perfection. How can sin-cursed people possibly have a personal relationship with a holy God? This is why Isaiah's first response to his vision of the holiness of God was to proclaim, "Woe is me, for I am ruined! Because I am a man of unclean lips, and I live among a people of unclean lips; for my eyes have seen the King, the LORD of hosts" (Isaiah 6:5).

Students of church history know that this is the concept that plagued Martin Luther. Verses like Romans 1:17 haunted him: "For in it the righteousness of God is revealed from faith to faith; as it is written, 'But the righteous man shall live by faith.'" How can anyone ever be righteous?

A SHALLOW SUBSTITUTE

Too often we address this perceived gap between our sin and God's standard of perfection with some form of self-righteousness. This may be why Pete loves to brag—to paint a thin coat of human accomplishment on a troubled heart. It may be why Faye is gripped with fear because she secretly wonders if her shortcomings have left her outside of God's compassionate provision. Dee's self-loathing could be connected to this challenge as she looks in the mirror and reminds herself of all her failures and misdeeds. In fact, each person in our circle probably struggles with some form of self-righteousness. Dealing with our lack of righteousness improperly is a problem that goes as far back as the Garden of Eden, where, after our first parents ate the forbidden fruit, they ran, hid, and tried to cover their shame.

How do you deal with your lack of perfection? Do you try to find ways to blame your failures on others? Do you drown the pain with another binge of alcohol? Do you turn up the noise of busyness and entertainment with the hope the emptiness will go away? The list of shallow options is practically endless.

AN AMAZING PROVISION

This is where the beauty of the gospel comes shining through in dazzling array. It is the sweetest vein in the multiple layers of the ice cream pie. In Christ, we receive both the forgiveness of our sin and the imputed righteousness of Christ. In other words, when you repent of your sin and trust Christ as Lord and Savior, the righteousness of Christ is placed on your account as a free gift of grace. When the heavenly Father looks at you, he does not see your failure, guilt, or endless shortcomings. Instead, he sees you clothed in the righteousness of his Son. Stop and think about what this means—*you are righteous.*

In chapter 5, we reviewed a passage that many students of Scripture consider to be the heart of the Bible, Romans 3:23-26. Our goal in that chapter was to consider what these verses teach us about redemption. As beautiful as it is to consider that Christ's blood cleanses us from our sin, that is only half the story. At the same time, Jesus' righteousness becomes ours. Read the passage again, this time viewing it through that lens:

> All have sinned and fall short of the glory of God, being justified as a gift by His grace through the redemption which is in Christ Jesus; whom God displayed publicly as a propitiation in His blood through faith. This was to demonstrate

His righteousness, because in the forbearance of God He passed over the sins previously committed; for the demonstration, I say, of His righteousness at the present time, so that He would be just and the justifier of the one who has faith in Jesus (Romans 3:23-26).

This is the biblical truth that brought Martin Luther to a saving knowledge of Jesus. He later wrote:

Night and day I pondered until I saw the connection between the justice of God and the statement that "the just shall live by his faith." Then I grasped that the justice of God is that righteousness by which *through grace and sheer mercy* God justifies us through faith. Thereupon I felt myself to be reborn and to have gone through open doors into paradise. The whole of Scripture took on a new meaning, and whereas before the "justice of God" had filled me with hate, now it became to me inexpressibly sweet in greater love. This passage of Paul became to me a gate to heaven.[2]

A DELIGHTFUL PICTURE

The prophet Zechariah wrote of a heavenly vision that pointed to this beautiful transaction. God showed him a high priest named Joshua standing before the angel of Lord, clothed in filthy garments, with Satan poised to accuse him of his failures. Then the Lord rebuked Satan for his accusations and instructed those standing around Joshua to

"Remove the filthy garments from him." Again he said to him, "See, I have taken your iniquity away from you and will clothe you with festal robes." Then I said, "Let them put a clean turban on his head." So they put a clean turban on his head and clothed him with garments, while the angel of the LORD was standing by (Zechariah 3:4-5).

That is what happens to us the moment we believe in Christ. Our filthy garments are removed, and we are clothed in the righteousness of God's Son. In the words of Paul, "He made Him who knew no sin to be sin on our behalf, so that we might become the righteousness of God in Him" (2 Corinthians 5:21).

Christian friend, positionally before our holy God, you are righteous. Do you believe what God says about you?

QUESTIONS FOR PERSONAL REFLECTION

1. Have you memorized Scripture verses about the righteousness of Christ being placed on you? If not, take the time to memorize 2 Corinthians 5:21.

2. What strands of self-righteousness do you see in your heart and life? How does the tendency to rely on self-righteousness manifest itself in your story?

3. What would be different about your daily life if you believed more comprehensively the truth that in Christ, you are righteous?

QUESTIONS FOR GROUP DISCUSSION

1. What practical strategies can you think of for replacing self-righteousness with the righteousness of Jesus?

2. What Christian hymns or contemporary songs emphasize the truth that you are righteous in Christ?

3. Come up with practical examples of how believing what God says about the believer's righteousness would change that believer's response to a specific problem or difficulty. If you are in a group, have everyone take turns coming up with answers.

CHAPTER 10

You Are Indwelled

S omething new started happening to me this week," Dee shared when her turn came to update the group. "I walked by the mirror and I still had that first instinct to think about my failures, my weight gain, and my messy hair. But right in the middle of those condemning thoughts, I began reviewing the biblical truths we've been studying together. I smiled as I thought about what God says about who I am in Christ—things like being loved, redeemed, adopted, forgiven, and united with Christ. Then I thought specifically about what we discussed in our last meeting—I am clothed with Christ's righteousness. Though I still battle not to believe those old lies, a profound sense of joy came over my heart that began defeating my typical self-loathing. I really believe God is helping me change—little by little."

Everyone responded positively to Dee's report and agreed that they, too, were in a battle to believe the Bible's truths instead of Satan's lies. They all were seeing concrete changes—each in different ways and at a different pace. Walt smiled and said, "I know what Grandpa would say right now. 'Children, that's the Holy Ghost working in you.'"

"Wow," Faye said. "I really believe that's true."

IN FULFILLMENT OF
A COMFORTING PROMISE

Do you remember the ice cream pie I mentioned in the previous chapter? The only problem with that illustration is that most of us have a limit for how many rich desserts we want to eat at any given time. That's not the case when it comes to the marvelous theological truths we've been considering in this book. God's Word has a way of both satisfying us and creating a hunger for a deeper understanding of what we're learning. This is certainly the case when it comes to the amazing truth that followers of Jesus Christ are indwelt by the Spirit of God.

One of the first places in Scripture where this topic is raised is with Jesus' disciples in John 14, a tender part of Christ's Upper Room Discourse just prior to his going to the cross. After foretelling Peter's threefold denial of him, Jesus looked at his followers and said, "Do not let your heart be troubled; believe in God, believe also in Me" (John 14:1). Isn't that just like our wonderful Savior? Even when he would soon be tortured and killed for our sin, his concern is for our troubled hearts. A few verses later, he gave a promise that has encouraged God's people for generations since:

> I will ask the Father, and He will give you another Helper, that He may be with you forever; that is the Spirit of truth, whom the world cannot receive, because it does not see Him or know Him, but you know Him because He abides with you and will be in you (verses 16-17).

You have to wonder what Peter must have thought about this promise after just hearing the startling news that he would soon deny Jesus multiple times. The Gospel of John ends with Peter's marvelous restoration, and soon thereafter, the promised Holy Spirit came upon the disciples on the Day of Pentecost. Peter then powerfully proclaimed the resurrected Christ to the crowds on that day (Acts 2:14-36) because the Holy Spirit was working in and through him.

This is why people like Dee, Faye, you, and me can anticipate spiritual change in ways we didn't think humanly possible. Yes, we will experience ups and downs, but we will also experience progressive victory in Christ. That's the point—one of the blessings of being in Christ is that we are indwelled by God's Spirit, who empowers us for our daily journey. Friend, do you believe what God's Word says about you and your progressive growth and victory through the Holy Spirit?

AS A GUARANTEE OF DIVINE PRODUCTIVITY AND PROTECTION

Another place in the Bible where this subject is discussed is 1 Corinthians 3:16-17. That is encouraging because the Corinthian church was famous for its immaturity and divisiveness. Yet Paul exhorted the Christians there to focus their attention on building on the foundation of Christ in a way that best prepared them for the coming judgment seat of Christ. After explaining that "each man's work will become evident; for the day will show it because it is to be revealed with fire, and the fire will test the quality of each man's work" (1 Corinthians 3:13), a few verses later, he asked:

> Do you not know that you are a temple of God and that the Spirit of God dwells in you? If any man destroys the temple of God, God will destroy him, for the temple of God is holy, and that is what you are (verses 16-17).

Even in their immature state, there was something about them that was more important than their failures, arguments, and past mistakes. In Christ, they were each temples of God indwelt by, as Walt's grandfather would so eloquently say, "the Holy Ghost himself." This is why they could have hope. They could build their lives on the foundation of Christ in a way that would someday be tested and found to be like gold, silver, and precious stones (1 Corinthians 3:12). The indwelling Holy Spirit would progressively make such a lifestyle possible.

Next, Paul layers on an additional implication of this provision.

Those who tried to destroy one of these temples would face God's judgment. The Holy Spirit not only empowers our growth, he divinely protects our existence.

TO MOTIVATE YOU TO PERSONAL PURITY

Paul raises this issue again a few chapters later when he is teaching the believers in Corinth about how to use their bodies to honor the Lord.

> Do you not know that your body is a temple of the Holy Spirit who is in you, whom you have from God, and that you are not your own? For you have been bought with a price: therefore glorify God in your body (1 Corinthians 6:19-20).

These verses hold out the incredible possibility that we as Christians can use our bodies in ways that can bring glory to God. Most of us would not have to think very long to assemble a list of all the ways we tend to displease God by what we do with our bodies (maybe I shouldn't have told you about that ice cream pie after all). However, our situation is not any more hopeless than the Corinthians were beyond the grip of God's transforming grace. The Holy Spirit's indwelling presence means that people like you and me can change in ways that no human being can do on their own.

TO HELP YOU AVOID IDOLATRY

Paul taught this church additional truths about the Holy Spirit's presence in the book of 2 Corinthians. There, as he taught them about the importance of maintaining pure relationships, he wrote:

> What agreement has the temple of God with idols? For we are the temple of the living God; just as God said, "I will dwell in them and walk among them; And I will be their God, and they shall be My people" (2 Corinthians 6:16).

The more we believe what God's Word says about the Holy Spirit's presence inside of us, the more natural it will be for us to avoid any form of idolatry that grips our hearts and lives. Paul is right—a temple of God has no agreement with idols. Acknowledging this aspect of our identity makes it easier to walk increasingly in ways that please him as the Holy Spirit transforms us more and more each day (2 Corinthians 4:16-18).

QUESTIONS FOR PERSONAL REFLECTION

1. How prominent of a role does the concept of the indwelling Spirit of God play in your daily thought process?

2. How should the fact the Holy Spirit dwells in you embolden you to address the areas in your life that need ongoing growth and change?

3. How important has it been to you to glorify God in your body because you are the temple of the Holy Spirit? What do you think it looks like for a person to glorify God?

QUESTIONS FOR GROUP DISCUSSION

1. Do you believe this aspect of the believer's identity—being indwelt and empowered by the Holy Spirit—receives the attention it deserves among Christians? Why or why not?

2. With a special emphasis on the verses we studied in John 14, how can this doctrine of the Spirit indwelling us bring calm to our troubled hearts?

3. Read Peter's sermon on the Day of Pentecost (Acts 2:14-36) out loud (if you're in a group, take turns reading the passage). What are some examples of how these words demonstrated the power of the indwelling Spirit?

CHAPTER 11

You Are a Worshipper

How did everyone's week go?" Faye asked as the group was taking their seats.

"Well, I did something different," Pete said.

Everyone recoiled a bit because of Pete's tendency to make prideful pronouncements. Yet this time his tone was different, and they wondered what Pete was about to say.

"That verse we studied from 2 Corinthians last week hit me hard," Pete said. "If I truly am indwelled by the Spirit, then why am I such an idol worshipper?"

"What do you mean?" Curt asked. "You have never brought any little statues in here and asked us to worship them with you."

"That may be true, but why have I spent so much of my life talking about my accomplishments?" Pete asked. "Why are there so many things at my house that are monuments to my achievements? Why am I so defensive when someone points out a weakness or trait I need to change? I've come to realize I've let my heart become crammed full with idols. So I packed up most of my trophies and am starting to replace them with reminders of what Christ has done for me. I want my life to be less about worshipping me and all about worshipping him."

GOD CREATED US AS WORSHIPPING BEINGS

Part of being made in the image of God are the abilities to think and reason. We were given the capacity to know truth and respond with choices that bring honor and glory to our Creator. This is why Paul's summary in Romans 1 is such a haunting analysis of the human condition apart from Christ: "They exchanged the truth of God for a lie, and worshiped and served the creature rather than the Creator, who is blessed forever. Amen" (verse 25).

One of the distinctive features of those of us who have placed our faith and trust in Christ is that we now live in ways that show how worthy we consider the Lord to be. For example, when God tested Abraham's faith by instructing him to take Isaac to a mountain and offering him as a sacrifice, this great patriarch described his actions to the onlooking servants by saying, "Stay here with the donkey, and I and the lad will go over there; and we will worship and return to you" (Genesis 22:5). One amazing detail in this story is that the verb "return" is plural. Abraham believed that God was completely worthy of his trust and obedience and that the Lord would keep his covenant promise regarding Isaac, even if that meant raising his slain son from the dead. The God of heaven was the one Abraham wanted he and Isaac to worship.

This issue is so central to our existence that God's very first command to his people stipulated, "You shall have no other gods before Me. You shall not make for yourself an idol, or any likeness of what is in heaven above or on the earth beneath or in the water under the earth. You shall not worship them or serve them" (Exodus 20:3-5).

WE POSSESS WORSHIPPING HEARTS

Our friend Pete might not have realized this, but his analysis of the root of his pride came from a famous passage in Ezekiel. The prophet records a day when a group of Israel's leaders came to receive guidance from the Lord, at which point God says,

Son of man, these men have set up their idols in their hearts and have put right before their faces the stumbling block of their iniquity. Should I be consulted by them at all? Therefore speak to them and tell them, "Thus says the Lord God, 'Any man of the house of Israel who sets up his idols in his heart, puts right before his face the stumbling block of his iniquity, and then comes to the prophet, I the Lord will be brought to give him an answer in the matter in view of the multitude of his idols, in order to lay hold of the hearts of the house of Israel who are estranged from Me through all their idols'" (Ezekiel 14:3-5).

The people of God had fallen far from God's design for them to worship him and from their obedience to the first commandment. This is why theologian John Calvin said that "the human heart is a perpetual idol factory."[3] Pete is correct. Sure, he doesn't worship small statues of stone or wood, but we all face the temptation to worship ourselves or some other object instead of the God of the Bible.

A FREQUENT TEST

The question of who or what we are worshipping in any given moment frequently arises in Scripture. This was a central focus of the book of Daniel, which reports that while many of the Israelites were worshipping false gods, some of God's children didn't. They recognized the test for their loyalty and faced it successfully. Rejoice and find hope in the words of Shadrach, Meshach, and Abednego:

O Nebuchadnezzar, we do not need to give you an answer concerning this matter. If it be so, our God whom we serve is able to deliver us from the furnace of blazing fire; and He will deliver us out of your hand, O king. But even if He does not, let it be known to you, O king, that we are not going to serve your gods or worship the golden image that you have set up (Daniel 3:16-18).

The greatest example of victory over the temptation to commit idolatry is when Satan took Jesus into the wilderness and offered him the kingdoms of the world if our Lord would fall down and worship him. Close your eyes and imagine the sin-shattering power of the Messiah's response: "Go Satan! For it is written, 'You shall worship the Lord your God, and serve Him only'" (Matthew 4:10).

A MARK OF OUR REDEMPTION

Paul raised this refrain when he described the followers of Christ at Thessalonica as those who had "turned to God from idols to serve a living and true God" (1 Thessalonians 1:9). That is why people like Pete, everyone else in the group, and you and I can have hope. A key aspect of our identity in Christ is that we worship the Lord in our hearts and lives in both "spirit and truth" (John 4:23).

Growing Christians seek to develop the habit of asking questions about their growth at any given moment—questions like:

- Who or what am I worshipping right now?
- Where am I seeking my joy and satisfaction?
- In whom am I placing my trust and allegiance?
- What is the identity of my functional god in this situation?

Asking such questions may lead to moments of repentance—times when we realize that we have allowed a belief, a person, or an object to take Christ's place in our heart and life. Thankfully, God stands ready with open arms of forgiveness when we recommit ourselves to worshipping him alone.

We can rejoice, then, over Pete's change of heart because he is choosing to believe what God says about him. As a result, he is setting aside his pride and focusing on what Christ has done for him.

QUESTIONS FOR PERSONAL REFLECTION

1. How often do you consider who or what you are worshipping?

2. What does worshipping Jesus look like in the practical moments of everyday life? How should worshipping Jesus impact your thoughts, desires, speech, and behavior?

3. What is your response to John Calvin's suggestion that if we do not direct ourselves with biblical truths, our hearts can become a perpetual idol factory?

QUESTIONS FOR GROUP DISCUSSION

1. What do you think would be true about the lifestyles of people who are consistent about worshipping Jesus?

2. What kinds of sinful behaviors can be traced to false worship?

3. What impact does our redemption have on our ability to worship well?

CHAPTER 12

You Are a Sinner

"A friend asked me the other day why I liked being in this group," Faye remarked.

"What did you say?" Andy asked.

"I told her that I enjoyed the growing authenticity of everyone in this circle. The more we talk about who we are in Christ, the easier it is to be honest about our failures and weaknesses. I used to blame my choices on external circumstances or other people, like I was simply a passive victim. But as I choose to more fully believe what God says about me, I feel less threatened by honestly acknowledging my responsibility in my struggles. I still have a long way to go, but I'm becoming more comfortable with being transparent about my sins."

THE IMPORTANCE OF WALKING IN THE LIGHT

Faye and her friends have reached an important point in their pursuit to believe and act on what God has said about them. In New Testament parlance, they are learning to allow the gospel to motivate them to *walk in the light*.

We learn about this important biblical concept in 1 John. The initial verses are very similar to John 1 and its emphasis on Christ being the light of the world. However, in the epistle, John develops the incredible truth that knowing Christ makes it possible for us to have greater fellowship with both God and people. In verse 3, he affirms, "What we have seen and heard we proclaim to you also, so that you too may have fellowship with us; and indeed our fellowship is with the Father, and with His Son Jesus Christ" (1 John 1:3). This is what every human being craves—a more intimate relationship with God and more meaningful relationships with other people.

Next, John explains the hindrance to achieving this condition, an approach to living he calls walking in darkness. He even goes so far as to suggest that "if we say that we have fellowship with Him and yet walk in the darkness, we lie and do not practice the truth" (verse 6). Could this play a role in explaining Andy's anger or Pete's pride? Could it explain the areas in which you and I struggle? Wouldn't it be terrible if we were living in a way that God would describe as walking in darkness, lying, and not practicing the truth?

Thankfully, whenever God's Word points out a problem, it also provides a superior alternative in Christ. This is when John introduces the concept of walking in the light: "If we walk in the Light as He Himself is in the Light, we have fellowship with one another, and the blood of Jesus His Son cleanses us from all sin" (verse 7).

This leaves the reader to wonder exactly what John means by this important phrase. Like so many other passages in Scripture, the answer is found by following the important principle of Bible study known as "just keep reading." Verses 8 and 10 leave no doubt about what John means by telling people like you and me to walk in the light:

- "If we say that we have no sin, we are deceiving ourselves and the truth is not in us" (verse 8).

- "If we say that we have not sinned, we make Him a liar and His word is not in us" (verse 10).

If we want to believe what God's Word says about us, we must daily acknowledge the uncomfortable truth that we still struggle with sin.

This does not discount the horrible abuses people may suffer or the sometimes-terrible pain of living in a sin-cursed world. But if we want genuine fellowship with God and others, we must have a willingness to admit our own sin. Light exposes, and God has given us the light of the gospel to help us honestly face those aspects of our inner and outer persons that still need to change.

THE TEST OF WALKING IN THE LIGHT

This would be a good time for you to pause and ask yourself if you are a person who walks in the light. You could even ask a loved one or friend to help evaluate you. Questions like these could lead to meaningful conversations:

- Do you think I have an open attitude toward admitting my sins?

- Am I a person who walks in the light in my relationship with you?

- Are there habits in my speech and behavior that make it harder for you to talk to me about needed changes?

- What could I do, or stop doing, that would help me walk in the light more faithfully in the days ahead?

Within 1 John 1, John has embedded a test. It is a well-known verse, perhaps the most oft-quoted words in the entire chapter, albeit rarely in their context: "If we confess our sins, He is faithful and righteous to forgive us our sins and to cleanse us from all unrighteousness" (verse 9). The principle is: Show me a person who is walking in the light, and I'll show you a person who regularly confesses sin to God and requests forgiveness of others.

THE BASIS OF WALKING IN THE LIGHT

All of us would say that living this way is hard. We don't like to admit our sins, and we look for all sorts of ways to deny this essential aspect of what Scripture says we should believe about ourselves. However, the gospel comes to our rescue yet again. The first two verses of 1 John 2 explain why this approach to life is attainable:

> My little children, I am writing these things to you so that you may not sin. And if anyone sins, we have an Advocate with the Father, Jesus Christ the righteous; and He Himself is the propitiation for our sins; and not for ours only, but also for those of the whole world (1 John 2:1-2).

Note carefully the two wonderful attributes of our Savior in these verses. First, he is our advocate with the Father. The word translated "advocate" means "attorney," as if Jesus is the one arguing our case. Yet he never argues on the basis of our own merit because we would always fall short. That is why John affirms that he is Jesus Christ the righteous. Our standing before God is not based on our righteousness, but on the imputed/shared righteousness of God's Son.

However, Jesus could not function in this role unless he was also our propitiation, or satisfaction. Our faith in his perfect sacrifice for our sins ensures that our standing before God is perfectly and eternally secure.

These two truths should motivate and empower us to be honest about our shortcomings. We do not have to be afraid that God will reject us for admitting what he already knows to be true. And even more importantly, his Son's shed blood on the cross has paved the way for our sin to be forgiven and our lives to be cleansed from all unrighteousness.

Faye is coming to believe these two truths, which will radically impact her relationships with God and other people. Will you choose to believe these two truths as well?

QUESTIONS FOR PERSONAL REFLECTION

1. How would you evaluate yourself on the issue of walking in the light?

2. Consider posing the questions on page 83 to trusted fellow believers who might be able to help determine how you're doing when it comes to walking in the light. What are the benefits of getting another person's perspective?

3. What specific steps could you take to more faithfully believe and act on what God says about this aspect of your identity?

QUESTIONS FOR GROUP DISCUSSION

1. Why is it so hard to walk in the light? What are some of the substitutes for living this way?

2. What is the relationship between the gospel truths articulated in 1 John 2:1-2 and the principle of walking in the light in 1 John 1:5-10?

3. Share examples of people you know who excel at this principle and how it impacts their relationships.

CHAPTER 13

You Are a Sufferer

Finally, the group's long-awaited day has come. A special guest had promised to join them today. Faye has baked her award-winning pumpkin bars, and Andy has supplied fresh apple cider from the local orchard.

As everyone enjoys their snacks and takes their seats, Walt enters with his grandfather, the Reverend William Cummings. He is exactly what many of the group members envisioned, a refined gentleman in his mid-eighties who bears a strong resemblance to his grandson. Walt is obviously proud of his grandpa and treats him with dignity and care.

Pastor Cummings's voice is deep, rich, and strong. There's also a twinkle in his eye that comes from a life that has learned to find joy from a supernatural source. He tells the group that he has been praying for them, and Faye suggests that everyone go around and update him on what they each have been working on since the group was formed.

"It is delightful to hear about the ways the Lord has been growing you," Pastor Cummings said. "It reminds me of what Paul said to the Philippians, that they should work out their own salvation with fear and trembling, 'for it is God who is at work in you, both to will and to work for His good pleasure.'[4] I am glad to hear that you are striving to believe and act on what God says about you."

Dee asked, "Pastor, could you tell us about your life story?"

The next half hour was filled with a mixture of sadness, victory, injustice, and deep faith. Pastor Cummings told about growing up in a segregated America where black persons were treated with indignity and bias. They were judged harshly because of the color of their skin and denied basic privileges and opportunities that many white people took for granted. Some of the stories he told and examples he gave were hard for the members of the group to hear. As they listened, their hearts were deeply moved.

Pastor Cummings also shared about times when he marched with others against injustice and fought for an America that was more in line with the principle of liberty and justice for all. "What sustained you through all of this?" Faye asked.

"It was my Jesus," Pastor Cummings replied. "This world is not my home, and I choose to find my identity in him. That includes a verse from the same book I mentioned a moment ago. 'To you it has been granted for Christ's sake, not only to believe in Him, but also to suffer for His sake'" (Philippians 1:29).

A RICH SUFFEROLOGY

Scripture is filled with affirmations that in this sin-cursed world in which we live, God's people will often suffer. It is instructive that even though the book of Philippians, which Pastor Cummings quoted, says much about the themes of joy and contentment, it also includes predictions that followers of Jesus will often experience deep heartache and pain.

Another example is Romans 8. At the end of one of the most extended discussions of progressive sanctification (Christian growth) anywhere in the New Testament (Romans 6–8), Paul challenged the children of God to know and believe that suffering will be an important aspect of the work God seeks to do in and through them.

Proof of Our Adoption

Paul told the Roman Christians that "the Spirit Himself testifies with our spirit that we are children of God, and if children, heirs also, heirs of God and fellow heirs with Christ, if indeed we suffer with Him" (Romans 8:16-17). Far from the so-called health-and-wealth theologies that suggest that problem-free living is available for those who simply have the right amount of faith, Scripture is clear that the Spirit himself will remind us regularly that suffering in this life is wrapped up in our identity in Christ.

For a Divine Purpose

Like everything our loving heavenly Father allows to occur in our lives, he has a purpose for suffering that is both beautiful and divine, which is why Paul concludes Romans 8:16-17 with a crucial purpose clause: "so that we may also be glorified with him." Pastor Cummings is proof of the power of this aspect of our identities. Responding well to suffering has refined him into a godly man whose life and character bring great glory to the Lord.

Requiring Careful Consideration

Paul went on to explain how he processes such challenging truths: "I consider that the sufferings of this present time are not worthy to be compared with the glory that is to be revealed in us" (verse 18). This concept is a key element in learning to believe what God says about you. You must carefully consider whether you truly believe and embrace Scripture's description of your identity. You are a sufferer. God has called and enabled you for this purpose.

Focusing Our Hope

When Pastor Cummings affirms that this world is not his home, he is articulating a belief that serves as an anchor to our souls when times are hard. Paul explained,

> We ourselves groan within ourselves, waiting eagerly for our adoption as sons, the redemption of our body. For in hope we have been saved, but hope that is seen is not hope;

for who hopes for what he already sees? But if we hope for what we do not see, with perseverance we wait eagerly for it (verses 23-25).

This does not mean that we don't stand up for justice and righteousness for ourselves and others whenever it is appropriate to do so. However, we understand that our ultimate hope is not in this world, but the next. We also rejoice in the hope that the blood of Jesus Christ alone makes this hope secure.

With a Divine Prayer Partner

Often our episodes of suffering seem difficult, if not impossible, to endure. In such moments, we have an opportunity to add yet another powerful way to think about ourselves. As we suffer, the Spirit is praying on our behalf.

In the same way the Spirit also helps our weakness; for we do not know how to pray as we should, but the Spirit Himself intercedes for us with groanings too deep for words; and He who searches the hearts knows what the mind of the Spirit is, because He intercedes for the saints according to the will of God (verses 26-27).

A godly man like Pastor Cummings did not produce that kind of character in his own strength and wisdom. He, like every follower of Jesus, has the Holy Spirit praying in ways we will never fully understand in this life. Imagine the third person of the Trinity being your prayer partner during a period of suffering. That is exactly what God says is true about you.

For Our Good and God's Glory

The next verses in Romans 8 are some of the best-known in this entire chapter:

We know that God causes all things to work together for good to those who love God, to those who are called according to His purpose. For those whom He foreknew, He also predestined to become conformed to the image of His Son (verses 28-29).

We can rejoice in the truth that even in times of suffering, our sovereign God can work such events for our spiritual good as we seek to be more conformed to the likeness of our Savior. Many of us look back to periods of intense trial and believe those were also the very events that provided the greatest opportunities for spiritual growth.

With a Divine Promise

The temptation during challenging times is to believe that God has abandoned us. This is why this marvelous passage ends with a powerful promise:

> In all these things we overwhelmingly conquer through Him who loved us. For I am convinced that neither death, nor life, nor angels, nor principalities, nor things present, nor things to come, nor powers, nor height, nor depth, nor any other created thing, will be able to separate us from the love of God, which is in Christ Jesus our Lord (verses 37-39).

This is your identity—a sufferer who is promised that not even the worst possible suffering can separate you from the love of God. You are a secure sufferer—secured in and by the love of Christ. Christ's promise is not the absence of suffering, but victory *in the midst* of suffering.

A SOBER REALITY

Every person in the group is filled with a mixture of sadness and admiration for Pastor Cummings, who has learned to believe what God's Word says about him—not just in some abstract fashion but in the course of his intense battles with injustice and profound suffering. Yet there he sits, with a twinkle in his eye, as if he knows better days are ahead.

Pete can't help but say, "Pastor Cummings, you really believe this about yourself, don't you? You face your suffering honestly as you cling to Christ to find eternal hope in the middle of life's worst trials."

"Yes, I do, young man," the pastor replied. "I surely do."

Everyone asks Pastor Cummings to join them for the next few sessions together. He smiles and says, "Well, that depends entirely, Ms. Faye, on whether I can expect any more of those pumpkin bars."

QUESTIONS FOR PERSONAL REFLECTION

1. What is your response to the important truth that God has called you to be a sufferer who clings to Christ in the midst of daily trials?

2. Do you prepare your heart with this principle ("I am a sufferer who must cling to Christ daily") each day, or do episodes of suffering tend to take you by surprise?

3. Do you know a person like Pastor Cummings, who has handled suffering well by facing it honestly and clinging tenaciously to Christ? What impact has that individual had on you and others?

QUESTIONS FOR GROUP DISCUSSION

1. Do you find the church to be an easy place to be honest about suffering? Why is such authenticity sometimes elusive for the people of God?

2. Describe the lifestyle of people who factor this aspect of their identity—suffering and clinging to Christ—into their daily outlook and choices.

3. How would your life be different if you remembered more consistently that part of your identity as a believer is to suffer in Christ's name?

CHAPTER 14

You Are a Believer

Everyone chuckles at what has just transpired. Out of appreciation that Pastor Cummings is going to meet with them again, but without thinking to coordinate with one another, they all brought appetizers or desserts to be sure their special guest had something to snack on while they talked.

"I guess we should have planned ahead better," Dee said sheepishly. "What are we going to do with all this food?"

Pastor Cummings gave her his trademark grin that was already becoming a favorite sign to the group. "Young lady," he said, "I have been a pastor most of my adult life. I know how God's people love to eat when they get together. A pastor's belt is like a leather fence around a chicken graveyard." They all laughed at the pastor's quick wit and joyful disposition.

Then Pete spoke up. "Pastor, I've thought a lot about the stories you told us last week. I have never had the privilege of talking to someone like you who has experienced such prejudice and racism firsthand. Honestly, I lost sleep over this because I know that I've said and done things toward people of other ethnicities that were harsh and sinful. I even asked God to forgive me and help me do better. What I do not understand is, how are you still willing to sit down and talk with people like me and even have such obvious joy in doing so?"

Pastor Cummings thought for a moment, then said, "Pete, I appreciate your honesty. This side of heaven, we all have a long way to go. A lot of it comes down to what I choose to believe."

YOUR CORE BELIEFS

An important aspect of being made in the image of God is the ability to choose your core beliefs. This is why even as early as the Garden of Eden, God began counseling Adam and Eve so that they had access to his truth and the opportunity to choose to believe what he said. This is also why, when Satan appeared in Genesis 3, his very first words contradicted and undermined God's counsel. The story of his insidious plot begins, "Now the serpent was more crafty than any beast of the field which the LORD God had made. And he said to the woman, 'Indeed, has God said…?'" (verse 1).

At that moment, Adam and Eve were given an opportunity to choose what they believed. Their failure to decide well plunged humanity into an everlasting struggle with whether we would believe God's truth or the world's lies (Romans 5:12-14). The writer of Hebrews would later pick up on this theme when he wrote, "Without faith it is impossible to please Him, for he who comes to God must believe that He is and that He is a rewarder of those who seek Him" (11:6). People like Pastor Cummings are able to live victoriously even when they face terrible trials because they have used their God-given capacity to believe what he says about them.

GOD'S CONTROL

I have had the privilege to serve as a biblical counselor for well over thirty years. Many of the men and women who come for counseling have experienced terrible injustice and abuse. Because of the generational effects of Adam and Eve's sin, we are broken people living in a broken world.

At some point, the issue of God's sovereignty must be brought into the conversation. Every person has to decide whether to believe the events that occur in our lives are outside of God's knowledge and control, or he sovereignly allows us to experience a mixture of blessings and trials to help conform us to the image of his Son.

Deciding what to believe can be a challenge to a person who has lost a loved one in an automobile accident or who has received a diagnosis of a terminal disease. Wise counselors seek the guidance of the Spirit as they minister biblical truths to hurting hearts with grace and compassion.

Those who choose to believe what God says will find affirmation in passages like Ephesians 1:11-12, where we are told that "we have obtained an inheritance, having been predestined according to His purpose who works all things after the counsel of His will, to the end that we who were the first to hope in Christ would be to the praise of His glory." The words "all things" can be challenging to believe when the pain is raw and the injustice is right before our eyes. Often, we process our beliefs through the lens of lament and authentic suffering. This draws us nearer to our sympathetic Savior, whose shed blood makes it possible to "receive mercy and find grace to help in time of need" (Hebrews 4:16).

You might want to pause and ask yourself whether you believe what God's Word says about his sovereign control over the events of your life. A joyful man like Pastor Cummings can simultaneously be honest about injustice *and* work toward better conditions for everyone while also embracing the pain of a broken world as a means of being drawn to closer fellowship with God.

GOD'S POWER

Paul then explained in Ephesians 1 that children of God have access to the same kind of power that raised Christ from the dead. Please pause and think about what that means, and whether you truly believe this aspect of what God says about you. Paul's exact words were given in the form of a prayer:

I pray that the eyes of your heart may be enlightened, so that you will know what is the hope of His calling, what are the riches of the glory of His inheritance in the saints, and what is the surpassing greatness of His power toward us who believe. These are in accordance with the working of the strength of His might which He brought about in Christ, when He raised Him from the dead and seated Him at His right hand in the heavenly places (verses 18-20).

I have the privilege of writing this book from my second-floor office at our church's Northend Community Center (NCC). This center is a project the Lord allowed us to accomplish in collaboration with the mayor, his city council, the United Way, and many other community leaders. We invited a number of existing secular nonprofits to have space in our building so we could share resources and serve our city together. On purpose, the NCC was built in a distressed neighborhood that has significant ethnic diversity because we believe God's people should be leaders in racial reconciliation. Some of our partners specifically serve men and women who are African-American or Latino.

To communicate our goal of building greater harmony in our community, we hired a street artist from Chicago to paint a large mural on the front of our building entitled "Better Together." The mural features the faces of men and women who have grown up in this neighborhood, many of whom have demonstrated vibrant faith in the face of terrible injustice. What I love about the mural is the dignity and inner strength that is evident in many of the faces. It is true that the resurrection power of our God is available to people like you and me even as we suffer. Friend, do you believe that about you?

GOD'S LOVE

The doctrines of God's sovereignty and power are not presented in Scripture in some sort of callous, impersonal fashion. Instead, the Bible calls upon us to believe and remember that our God deeply loves us. This is why Paul prayed in this way for the Ephesians:

...that Christ may dwell in your hearts through faith; and that you, being rooted and grounded in love, may be able to comprehend with all the saints what is the breadth and length and height and depth, and to know the love of Christ which surpasses knowledge, that you may be filled up to all the fullness of God (Ephesians 3:17-19).

Your core beliefs have the capacity to lead you toward the Lord and greater Christlikeness even in the midst of pain and heartache, or drive you far away from him. There's a reason Pastor Cummings has that twinkle in his eye even though he fully recognizes this world is deeply marred by sin. Unlike Adam and Eve, he has chosen his core beliefs wisely.

QUESTIONS FOR PERSONAL REFLECTION

1. Make a list of your core beliefs. How do those ideas shape and direct you on a daily basis?

2. What influences are present in your life that tempt you to believe ideas about yourself and your world that are untrue?

3. How do friendships, culture, music, and entertainment factor into this discussion? Do your choices in these areas make it easier or harder to believe what God says about you?

QUESTIONS FOR GROUP DISCUSSION

1. Review the story of Adam and Eve in Genesis 3. What core beliefs did they have that ended up leading them astray?

2. What are some of the core beliefs that should guide every follower of Christ?

3. Using a Bible concordance, take time to look up the usage of words like *believe* and *believer* in the Bible. What verses especially stand out to you, and why?

CHAPTER 15

You Are a Thinker

P astor Cummings, what you're teaching us about our core beliefs is very helpful," Andy said. "I want to spend less time focusing on the choices of those around me and more time on what my angry responses say about what I truly believe. That helps me to remember that God created me as a human being with the ability to choose what I believe."

Pastor Cummings nodded. "That is tremendous, Andy. I think you will find it liberating when you place the bulk of your attention on evaluating and changing yourself, not on someone or something outside of the realm of your responsibility or control."

"But can you help me understand something?" Andy asked. "Your story of facing racism and discrimination as a black pastor makes me sad, frustrated, and angry. How did you access and act on your core beliefs in the middle of circumstances that brought you and those you loved such pain? I don't know how to do that."

Pastor Cummings smiled. "Andy, you are a thoughtful and honest man. I certainly did not handle every situation in my past perfectly. However, I learned early on that not only did God create us as believers, but also as thinkers."

"I'm not sure I understand the difference," said Andy. Others in the group nodded, wanting to know more as well.

"Think of it like this," Pastor Cummings said. "Your core beliefs are like the food in your refrigerator. Your thoughts are the specific ingredients you choose to remove at any given moment to make your next meal. It is critical that you select correct, biblical thoughts about whatever is happening around you. The good news is that in the power of the Spirit, you can learn to think wisely in the heat of the moment. The meal that results, and by that I mean your words and actions, can then bring God glory."

AN UPHILL BATTLE

Pastor Cummings is describing yet another essential aspect of our identity: We are thinkers. Wise people learn to carefully ask themselves questions like, *What am I thinking right now? Are these thoughts honoring to the Lord? Will the thoughts I'm choosing in this moment lead me to speak and behave in ways that please God?*

Paul explained the significance of the struggle we face in one of the most informative passages on Christian growth in the entire New Testament—Romans 6–8. In Romans 7:19, he made the stunning admission, "For the good that I want, I do not do, but I practice the very evil that I do not want." Only a person secure in his identity in Christ (Romans 6:1-23) could make such an honest statement. Then he said,

> I find then the principle that evil is present in me, the one who wants to do good. For I joyfully concur with the law of God in the inner man, but I see a different law in the members of my body, waging war against the law of my mind and making me a prisoner of the law of sin which is in my members (Romans 7:21-23).

This is the precise point Pastor Cummings was making. It is one thing to have core beliefs that align with the Word of God in a quiet moment of reflection. However, it requires an entirely different kind of discipline to learn to formulate and choose specific thoughts that are consistent with your biblical core beliefs when the arrows of trial, pain, and disappointment are flying at you.

We all know what it's like to fail in ways that make us say what Paul said in Romans 7:19. What we said or did in our moment of failure was completely inconsistent with what we proclaim to believe. The war is real, and the disconnect between our core beliefs and our thoughts and choices in the middle of a trial can be devastating. Too often we're so focused on what others are doing that we neglect to remember that God has made us thinkers. We do not have to respond in sinful and predictable ways that only make matters worse.

THE GOSPEL TO THE RESCUE

The good news that comes next in Romans 8 is like fresh water to a parched soul:

> The law of the Spirit of life in Christ Jesus has set you free from the law of sin and death. For what the law could not do, weak as it was through the flesh, God did: sending His own Son in the likeness of sinful flesh and as an offering for sin, He condemned sin in the flesh (verses 2-3).

Not only have we been created with the ability to choose specific thoughts in any given moment, but the power of the shed blood of Jesus makes it possible for us to align those thought choices with our biblical core beliefs.

Paul describes this process beautifully in the next verses:

> Those who are according to the flesh set their minds on the things of the flesh, but those who are according to the Spirit, the things of the Spirit. For the mind set on the flesh is death, but the mind set on the Spirit is life and peace (verses 5-6).

This might be a good time for you to pause and reflect on how much emphasis you place on this aspect of your identity. Do you tend to evaluate yourself in light of what others have done to you, or through the lens of the incorrect thoughts you have chosen in response to what occurred? What would be different if you spent more energy on choosing wise, biblical thoughts in the heat of the battle?

THE IMPORTANCE OF CHOOSING
YOUR THOUGHTS WISELY

Thankfully, Scripture even offers us specific filters to test and guide our choices. Using Pastor Cummings's refrigerator metaphor, think of God's Word as being like a recipe book that helps you choose ingredients from your core beliefs that will produce a masterful and delicious meal. For example, in Philippians 4:8-9 we read this:

> Brethren, whatever is true, whatever is honorable, whatever is right, whatever is pure, whatever is lovely, whatever is of good repute, if there is any excellence and if anything worthy of praise, dwell on these things. The things you have learned and received and heard and seen in me, practice these things, and the God of peace will be with you (Philippians 4:8-9).

These words should give us great hope because they demonstrate that we can control what we choose to think at any given moment. Thoughts that do not meet these important criteria can be replaced with ones that do. We do not have to allow "whatever pops into our minds" to remain there. Because of the power of the gospel working in and through us, we can and must choose to dwell only on thoughts that honor the Lord—thoughts that are true, honorable, right, pure, lovely, of good repute, excellent, and worthy of praise.

THE LONG-TERM IMPACT
OF THINKING LIKE CHRIST

"Pastor Cummings, I marvel at how refined, dignified, and peaceful you are," Faye remarked. "If I had faced a fraction of the injustice you've suffered, I think I would be bitter and defeated. You've taught us an important practical key to living victoriously in a sin-cursed world."

"Sweet sister," Pastor Cummings said, "at one time, this country said a man like me should be considered three-fifths human. I have been called demeaning names and treated as if the color of my skin rendered me ignorant and inferior. But I have determined to try to believe what God has said about me. I am a thinker, and in the power of the Holy Ghost, I can select thoughts about me and others each and every day that are consistent with what the Bible says. Doing this consistently has been a struggle and continues to be, but there is incredible peace and joy that comes from choosing my thoughts well, and living like the man God created me to be."

QUESTIONS FOR PERSONAL REFLECTION

1. How disciplined are you about evaluating the nature of your thoughts at any given moment?

2. What difficult moments did you experience this past week? What were you thinking before, during, and after these episodes? Did your thoughts meet the test of Philippians 4:8-9?

3. What habitual thought patterns will take you in the wrong direction? When you find yourself thinking negative thoughts, what steps can you take to reverse course mentally?

QUESTIONS FOR GROUP DISCUSSION

1. Did you find the information in this chapter helpful, challenging, sobering, or something else? Explain your answer.

2. Who comes to mind when you think of words like *refined*, *dignified*, and *peaceful*? What role do you believe that person's thought choices play in their ongoing character development?

3. What practical steps can a person take to be a better steward of this aspect of our identity—choosing our thoughts according to God's Word in response to our situations?

CHAPTER 16

You Long Deeply

Faye was thinking quickly, and it was clear she was using her engineering skills to process carefully what the group had been discussing. When there was a break in the conversation, she said, "Pastor Cummings, I'm so glad you're giving your time to help us. You've been such a blessing. Are there other aspects about my identity that might help me overcome the fears that so often grip my heart?"

The pastor thought for a moment, then said, "Faye, perhaps it is time for us to consider the red-button question." This caught everyone's attention, and they all blurted out at once, "The what?"

"Faye, if I had a magic red button on the arm of my chair that could make everything just the way you desired, what would you want to be different for you after I pushed it?"

"Oh, I know what I want the most. I want a guarantee of no health problems, a safe neighborhood, and a daughter-in-law who allows me to see my grandchildren whenever I wish. I long for a life like this and am so afraid it will never happen."

"Now I think we are really onto something," Pastor Cummings smiled. "God created us with the capacity to long deeply. This is a core aspect of our identity. Our innermost longings either move us toward the Lord in gospel-centered trust or move us away from him in human-centered fear and idolatry. It is important to learn what God says about what we want."

JUST LIKE A DEER

As Pastor Cummings said, another key aspect of our identity is our desires. Discern what you want in a given situation, and you will have revealed what is occurring in your heart. Your desires are an indicator of the steps you are about to take in response to whatever is happening around you. The principle is illustrated powerfully in Psalm 42:1-2: "As the deer pants for the water brooks, so my soul pants for You, O God. My soul thirsts for God, for the living God; when shall I come and appear before God?"

We are not simply told in a sterile, academic fashion that our hearts are filled with deep longings. Instead, we are directed to an animal that we all love to see—a beautiful deer. We can imagine her running through a field in search of cool water to satisfy her overwhelming thirst. We can hear her breathe and feel her heart beating. Then God says, "I created you with the ability to long deeply, just like this panting deer."

Part of the encouragement of Psalm 42 is the principle that people like you and me can learn to order our desires in a way that moves us toward the Lord. The writer speaks about the nature of his heart and his desire to commune with God in corporate worship. As verses 3-5 indicate, he is in a position where he is unable to join the Lord's people and his enemies are seeking to undermine his faith. He could have easily chosen a desire that was more focused on temporal relief or sinful satisfaction. But this godly man knew that he needed to choose the object of his affection wisely. Imagine this Old Testament saint faithfully affirming, "My soul pants for You, O God."

SO EASILY CORRUPTED

Like everything that God has created in and for us, our sin can twist and distort the Lord's purposes. Careful students of the Bible find this principle in many of the key passages about how Christians change and grow. For example, Paul explained to the Ephesians, "Among them we too all formerly lived in the lusts of our flesh, indulging the desires of the flesh and of the mind, and were by nature children of wrath, even as the rest" (Ephesians 2:3). John made a similar observation when he wrote:

> Do not love the world nor the things in the world. If anyone loves the world, the love of the Father is not in him. For all that is in the world, the lust of the flesh and the lust of the eyes and the boastful pride of life, is not from the Father, but is from the world. The world is passing away, and also its lusts; but the one who does the will of God lives forever (1 John 2:15-17).

Wise followers of Christ develop the habit of asking in any given situation, "What am I wanting right now, and is this a desire that God can bless?"

A FUNDAMENTAL ASPECT OF OUR SPIRITUAL GROWTH PROCESS

Perhaps the passage that best showcases the power of our desires from a process perspective is James 1:14-15: "Each one is tempted when he is carried away and enticed by his own lust. Then when lust has conceived, it gives birth to sin; and when sin is accomplished, it brings forth death."

James is using a metaphor from the world of hunting and fishing. He likens our desires to bait that has the ability to draw us away and entice us. As you consider the nuances of your own desires, listen for thoughts that begin with words like, "I want" or "I need" or "I deserve" or "I must have." It's amazing how often we allow a sinful desire to take root in us and then begin a pursuit that leads to sinful actions and their disastrous consequences.

To complicate matters, it's possible for a desire to be legitimate, but if you want it too much, it can easily become an illegitimate lust or idol.

That is what Faye has experienced. Her desires are legitimate, but to ensure they don't pull her away from God, she needs to see her desires as opportunities to draw closer to the Lord. She could say, for example, "I would like to have good health, but if I don't, I know my good God can use medical problems to draw me closer to him." Or, "I would prefer to live in a safer neighborhood, but I will use the challenges of my community as an opportunity to pray for the salvation of those who live around me." Or, "I wish my daughter-in-law would be more gracious, but because I cannot control that, I want to use this disappointment as an opportunity to commune more with my Savior, who will never leave me nor forsake me." The distance between "I must" and "I would like to have" can be enormous. It's also often the difference between a longing heart that pants for God and a lustful heart that seeks lesser substitutes. It's the difference between a desire and a demand.

REDEEMABLE BY THE BLOOD OF CHRIST

Think back to what Ephesians 2:3 says about the power of our lusts. Then look at Paul's very next words in Ephesians 2:4-5: "But God, being rich in mercy, because of His great love with which He loved us, even when we were dead in our transgressions, made us alive together with Christ (by grace you have been saved)."

God created us with the capacity to desire deeply. Sin can warp and distort our desires so that we twist them into demands. Salvation redeems our capacity to desire deeply so that in the power of Christ, we can learn to cultivate desires that please the Lord and move us closer to him in whatever circumstance we are facing. We can be like that beautiful deer that pants for the water brooks. We can be like Faye, who wants to point her desires toward the Lord and what he graciously chooses to provide. Knowing and honoring Christ can become the ultimate desire of our heart—more important than anything else we might want in this life.

QUESTIONS FOR PERSONAL REFLECTION

1. How often do you stop and consider the nature of your desires in a given situation?

2. List and identify legitimate desires you have that sometimes become sinful because you want them too much—they morph from desires to demands.

3. What steps can you take each day to order your desires so that pursuing and pleasing the Lord has first place in your heart?

QUESTIONS FOR GROUP DISCUSSION

1. What are some of the garden-variety desires that too often become idols in our hearts?

2. How does the process described in James 1:14-15 work out practically? "Test drive" several scenarios in which people's chosen desires entice and draw them away. In what sense does this often end, as James teaches, in sin and death?

3. How can we as Christians do a better job of guarding our hearts in this all-important area of surrendering our desires to the Lord?

CHAPTER 17

You Are Volitional

As the group gathered for their next meeting, there was excitement in the air. The previous week, Pastor Cummings had encouraged everyone to look for specific ways to apply what they had been studying and be ready to share real-life examples.

Curt's response was representative of what the others planned to share. "Believing what God's Word says about me has been transformational," he began. "I had a tough day at work on Tuesday, and when I sat down for dinner, I did not like the meal Carla prepared. I had an entire set of criticisms on the tip of my tongue, and then something amazing happened."

"Can I guess what it was?" Andy asked. "Because I think I have a couple of experiences that are similar to yours."

"Sure Andy," Curt smiled. "Go for it."

"You caught yourself before speaking foolishly and asked God to help you analyze what was going on inside of you," said Andy.

"Bingo," Curt replied. "What humbled me was that I quickly realized my core beliefs, my chosen thoughts in the moment, and my desires were all displeasing to God. Thankfully, the Lord allowed me to turn all of that around before I said anything mean and spiteful to Carla."

"Dee, would you please lead us in prayer and thank God for what Curt just shared?" Pastor Cummings asked. "This is a great example of him realizing that the issue was not what Carla had prepared for supper, but the condition of the heart that Curt brought to the meal. He believed what God said about him."

After Dee finished, everyone looked at each other with a sense of satisfaction and joy at the work the Lord was doing in and through them. They knew they still had a long way to go, but it was exciting to hear about the changes that were taking place in their lives.

Dee felt the moment was right for her to ask a question that had been on her heart for some time. "Pastor, as a Hispanic woman, people have often treated me as if I'm not as intelligent as others, or as important or valuable. You have told us of similar abuses you faced as an African-American man. Yet you went on to study for the ministry and become a respected leader of a church congregation and the local community. How did you do that?"

"Dee, it saddens me that you have ever been made to feel less knowledgeable or worthwhile because of the color of your skin. In our short time together, I know those things are not true—you are a sweet sister in Christ whom we highly value."

Pastor Cummings paused, then continued. "But you are right. Many people have discredited me because of the color of my skin. They have acted as if I was ignorant and morally deficient, unworthy of participation in their white man's society."

"So, how did you overcome that?" Pete asked. "It seems like you had so much stacked against you."

"An important element was choosing to believe what God said about me. The color of my skin had nothing to do with my identity as a man of God. He made me to be volitional—to make choices each day that honored him and reflected his image in me. I came to believe that the choices I made, if focused on following the Lord and his Word, were as significant and honoring to God as anyone else, regardless of the color of my skin."

A PIVOTAL DAY FOR GOD'S PEOPLE

There is a crucial statement recorded in the Old Testament that highlights the importance of the choices we make. It appears at the end of the book of Joshua, when Israel's great leader was preparing God's people for their responsibilities in the promised land:

> Fear the LORD and serve Him in sincerity and truth; and put away the gods which your fathers served beyond the River and in Egypt, and serve the LORD. If it is disagreeable in your sight to serve the LORD, choose for yourselves today whom you will serve: whether the gods which your fathers served which were beyond the River, or the gods of the Amorites in whose land you are living; but as for me and my house, we will serve the LORD (Joshua 24:14-15).

Joshua could have addressed these men and women in ways that would have diminished their responsibility and privilege at that moment. However, he wanted them to understand and believe an essential aspect of their identity—they had the capacity, in God's power, to make the right choice about the direction they would go.

Over the course of his life, Pastor Cummings found himself at similarly critical junctures many times. He could have believed the voices of those who treated him as if he were inferior and unable to make wise and purposeful choices. He could have focused on all the inequalities he faced and become an angry, bitter man. Instead, he made a habit of embracing his responsibility to make wise choices and trusting the Lord to direct his steps.

You and I are faced with challenging choices as well. We may be tempted to believe those who say we do not measure up or that we are powerless, hopeless victims in a meaningless existence. Yet God's Word paints an entirely different picture. We are volitional beings who can make godly choices that honor him regardless of the negative people and circumstances around us. We can know dignity, purpose, and even joy when we believe and act on this aspect of our identity.

THE POSSIBILITY AND IMPORTANCE
OF CHOOSING WISELY AND WELL

The people who received Joshua's challenge responded with this courageous affirmation:

> Far be it from us that we should forsake the LORD to serve other gods; for the LORD our God is He who brought us and our fathers up out of the land of Egypt, from the house of bondage, and who did these great signs in our sight and preserved us through all the way in which we went and among all the peoples through whose midst we passed. The LORD drove out from before us all the peoples, even the Amorites who lived in the land. We also will serve the LORD, for He is our God (Joshua 24:16-18).

You can imagine their excitement as they raised their voices to proclaim their choice to serve the Lord their God. Of course, there were many days in subsequent biblical history when they and their descendants wavered from this direction. But their nation would one day produce a Messiah, the holy Son of God who would face a series of choices on earth and, in each case, come out victoriously. The writer of Hebrews would later say of him:

> Since we have a great high priest who has passed through the heavens, Jesus the Son of God, let us hold fast our confession. For we do not have a high priest who cannot sympathize with our weaknesses, but One who has been tempted in all things as we are, yet without sin. Therefore let us draw near with confidence to the throne of grace, so that we may receive mercy and find grace to help in time of need (4:14-16).

This means that in every situation we face, whether big or small, our Savior stands ready to help lead and empower us to make choices that please and honor God. Choose to believe that you are volitional—that you have a will to choose God's way and be empowered by God's Spirit—and, that with the blessing of God, you can use this capacity well.

QUESTIONS FOR PERSONAL REFLECTION

1. Why is it so important to recognize that the choices you make each day have such a great impact on what happens in your life?

2. Are you glad God created you as a volitional being? How does this truth provide hope? How does it provide responsibility?

3. What is the relationship between our volition and the person and work of Jesus Christ as described in Hebrews 4:14-16?

QUESTIONS FOR GROUP DISCUSSION

1. What are some examples in Scripture of people who made wise choices and people who did not?

2. Where does the power of the gospel fit into this discussion?

3. Describe the lifestyle of a person who recognizes the importance of his or her choices when it comes to everyday living.

CHAPTER 18

You Are Emotional

Grandpa," Walt said, "I understand what you mean about focusing on the importance of making godly decisions regardless of your circumstances or the behavior of others. I watched you live that way as I was growing up.

"What intrigued me," he continued, "was the way you handled your emotions. Everything you did was done with passion, but it never appeared to be irrational or out of control. Where do our feelings fit into what we are learning?"

"I am glad that is the way you remember it, Walt," Pastor Cummings said. "I confess there were many times when my emotions got the best of me. But I tried to believe what God's Word says about this area of my life as well. The Lord created us with the capacity to feel an entire range of emotions. My goal was to let Scripture guide the way I exercised this important aspect of who God created me to be."

AVOIDING THE DITCHES

In theology and in many other areas of life, balance, as the old saying goes, is "that elusive point I pass on the way to my next extreme." Here in Indiana, where I pastor, we often speak about avoiding the ditches on both sides of the road as we try to navigate our approach to various topics and decisions.

One ditch we want to avoid is that of believing emotions are always bad. There are some who say that we should never express, trust, or value our emotions. And there are those who say we shouldn't allow ourselves to "get emotional," as if doing so is automatically a bad thing.

The problem with this perspective is that it fails to consider that God created us with the ability to feel joy, sorrow, anger, disappointment, and other emotions. The Lord declared this capacity to be "very good" when he summarized his evaluation of the way we were made (Genesis 1:31).

Another problem with the "emotions are always bad" position is that Scripture tells us Christ himself experienced emotions—we see times when he was sorrowful (John 11:35), angry (Mark 3:5), joyful (Hebrews 12:2), or grieved (Matthew 26:38). He expressed these and many other emotions without sinning in any way (Hebrews 4:15).

The ditch on the other side is believing that our emotions should not and cannot be guided, directed, or controlled in any way, shape, or form. Those who function in this extreme not only express their emotions, they live by them. Every other aspect of how God created them is subservient to how they're feeling in the moment. Their lives are often emotional roller coasters that travel from a blast of anger to an expression of exuberance and back again. People who live around such individuals must deal with the exhausting pressure of seemingly endless unpredictability.

EXPRESSING OUR EMOTIONS MORE FULLY

I encourage you to pause and consider which of these extremes you tend to lean toward when it comes to the way you express your God-given emotions. My experience in counseling is that people split about evenly into either category. Another interesting dynamic is that individuals often marry spouses who handle their feelings in the exact opposite extreme as they do. To say that this often leads to rather interesting counseling sessions would be an understatement. The good news is that Scripture can help a husband and wife, or any person or group of persons, learn to find biblical balance in this all-important area of their lives.

If you tend to be an "all emotions are bad and should therefore always be avoided" person, a good place to start would be to study the many Psalms of Lament. For example, you could read passages like Psalm 10 or Psalm 13 out loud. As you do so, pay attention not only to the writer's words, but the tone of voice and emotional component of what is being communicated. When we practice biblical lament, we are authentically communicating our feelings of anger, fear, disappointment, and dread to the Lord himself.

Consider how Christ followed this pattern in the Garden of Gethsemane prior to going to the cross when he said to three of his disciples, "My soul is deeply grieved, to the point of death; remain here and keep watch with Me" (Matthew 26:38). He then walked a bit further, fell on his face, and prayed, "My Father, if it is possible, let this cup pass from Me; yet not as I will, but as You will" (Matthew 26:39). No wonder the Old Testament predicted that the Messiah would be "a Man of sorrows, and acquainted with grief" (Isaiah 53:3). When you and I choose to honestly express the way we are feeling to God, we can do so in a Christlike manner without being sinful.

GOVERNING OUR EMOTIONS WITH GOD'S WORD

For those who lean toward the "unbridled emotions" side of the equation, we don't even have to leave Gethsemane to find helpful instruction. Matthew tells us that when Judas comes with a mob to arrest Jesus, one of Jesus' disciples (identified as Peter in John 18:10) "reached and drew out his sword, and struck the slave of the high priest and cut off his ear" (Matthew 26:51).

In contrast, Christ was the perfect example of controlling his emotions with biblical truth when he said,

> Put your sword back into its place; for all those who take up the sword shall perish by the sword. Or do you think

that I cannot appeal to My Father, and He will at once put at My disposal more than twelve legions of angels? How then will the Scriptures be fulfilled, which say that it must happen this way? (verses 52-54).

That is the secret to handling one's emotions in a way that honors the Lord. We must evaluate our feelings at any given moment with the truth of God's Word. When our emotions are in line with Scripture, we should express them fully. When they contradict God's instructions in the Bible, we should refuse to continue to go down that destructive path. Instead, we should ask God to help us express our emotions in ways that are more pleasing to him.

SEEING THIS BALANCE
IN OUR SWEET PASTOR

"Walt," Pastor Cummings said, "I am glad your recollection of my life and ministry is that I was passionate about what I did. I hope the way I loved my wife and your parents and all of you grandchildren was characterized by a kind of emotional love that was joyful and infectious. I hope as you listened to me preach, you observed a passionate love for Jesus that made you long to love him too. And as you saw me lead our church family in community endeavors to bring about racial justice and harmony in our country, I hope you saw a deep commitment born out of strong emotions that were being directed by biblical truth."

He paused, then said, "But Walt, I also hope that you saw a man who was more like Jesus in the garden and less like Peter. I always wanted the Scriptures to govern the way I expressed my emotions. This is what helped me avoid becoming a bitter, impulsive man. I am thankful that to whatever degree I succeeded in this endeavor, it was Jesus who made it possible."

QUESTIONS FOR PERSONAL REFLECTION

1. Of the two emotional ditches discussed in this chapter, which do you lean toward?

2. What are some ways you can be more like Jesus in the Garden of Gethsemane, and less like Peter?

3. Of the primary people in your life, which persons stand out as being the most balanced in the way they handle their emotions? How does this impact their lives and relationships?

QUESTIONS FOR GROUP DISCUSSION

1. Give some examples from God's Word of people who handled their emotions well and people who did not.

2. What are some other ways Jesus was a perfect example of "power under control"?

3. As you consider people in contemporary culture, who stands out as examples of the two emotional extremes discussed in this chapter? Who stands out as being appropriately balanced in the ways they handle their emotions?

CHAPTER 19

You Are an Actor

M s. Faye, this strawberry cheesecake is creating a real dilemma in my soul," said Pastor Cummings. "I can't decide if I like this better than your delectable pumpkin bars. The problem is, my initial test sample has completely disappeared from this plate."

Faye smiled. "In the name of scientific advancement, how about I serve you another piece? That first one was rather small." By now everyone in the group had come to know and appreciate the pastor's quick wit, so no one was surprised when he said, "Well, I suppose I should, for the sake of science."

"Seriously, Faye," Dee said, "this is unusually good. What is your secret?"

"Y'all are making me blush," said Faye. "But I have always liked this dessert too. I think it's a combination of a wonderful recipe passed down from my grandmother along with fresh ingredients right from my garden or local market. I also make it with lots of love, which I know may sound corny, but when I am baking, I actually think about how much I adore and appreciate the people who will be enjoying the final product."

"Well, Faye," Pastor Cummings said, "the proof of that is in the pudding, as they say." Then he looked around at the group. "Isn't that just what we have been studying together? When you select the right ingredients from your core beliefs, your desires, your patterns of thinking, and your emotions, the behavioral choices that result can be absolutely delicious."

THE REASON WE GUARD OUR HEARTS

We have spent the last several chapters examining various ways the Bible describes what takes place within us. This information brings both hope and responsibility. On the one hand, with the help of your chosen beliefs and your thoughts, desires, and emotions, you can avoid being ruled by your circumstances and the choices made by others around you. You do not have to view yourself as a passive victim with a meaningless existence. On the other hand, you must take responsibility for ordering the various aspects of your heart well.

The next logical question is, to what end? Pastor Cummings is not far off when he suggests that the proof is in the pudding. Ultimately, our behavior reveals what is occurring inside. This is why King Solomon taught, "Watch over your heart with all diligence, for from it flow the springs of life" (Proverbs 4:23). Each day, we all decide to act in certain ways. We must choose to believe what the Lord says about the importance of cultivating godly behavior.

THINKING ABOUT BEHAVIOR
REQUIRES BALANCE AS WELL

Just as we learned in chapter 18 with regard to emotions, there are two ditches on either side of the road when it comes to how we behave. Some of us may have grown up in environments that were behavioristic. We were given a list of dos and don'ts without much focus on the inner man behind the actions. This is a very short walk to creating a Pharisaical lifestyle, which almost always runs out of gas. Parents who seek to raise their children using this approach are often disappointed in the long run. We must always consider the condition of our heart as we seek to behave in ways that please the Lord.

The ditch on the other side is thinking that God is unconcerned with our behavioral choices. People at this extreme are comfortable talking about topics like grace, the inner workings of the gospel, or the finer points of theology, but they rarely want to discuss the behavioral expectations that God places on his children in his Word.

The correct balance is a well-cultivated heart that results in a life of growing obedience and godly character. With that in mind, the Lord's instructions about our behavior give us reason for hope because we view biblical living to be as delicious as a piece of Ms. Faye's delightful baked strawberry cheesecake.

PUTTING ON THE FRUIT OF THE SPIRIT

Lest anyone consider such an emphasis to be legalistic, please keep in mind that the book of Galatians is the epistle that most directly confronts the sin of legalism. Yet it also contains clear expectations from God regarding the way we choose to act each day. After an extended discussion about walking in the Spirit and being led by the Spirit, Paul wrote,

> Now the deeds of the flesh are evident, which are: immorality, impurity, sensuality, idolatry, sorcery, enmities, strife, jealousy, outbursts of anger, disputes, dissensions, factions, envying, drunkenness, carousing, and things like these, of which I forewarn you, just as I have forewarned you, that those who practice such things will not inherit the kingdom of God. But the fruit of the Spirit is love, joy, peace, patience, kindness, goodness, faithfulness, gentleness, self-control; against such things there is no law (Galatians 5:19-23).

These are the "issues of life" that Solomon spoke of in Proverbs 4:23. God wants his children to believe that we are responsible for our actions. We can either practice the deeds of the flesh or put on the fruit of the Spirit.

Consider how much focus you place on your behavioral choices on a given day. Scripture emphasizes this matter on nearly every page. Yes, we are saved by grace alone apart from works, and we should rejoice in this rich spiritual reality (Ephesians 2:8-9). But as Paul said in the very next verse, "We are His workmanship, created in Christ Jesus for good works, which God prepared beforehand so that we would walk in them" (verse 10).

BRINGING THE INGREDIENTS TOGETHER

After challenging the Christians in Galatia to put off the deeds of the flesh and put on the fruit of the Spirit, Paul concluded with words that tie together what we've learned up to this point: "Now those who belong to Christ Jesus have crucified the flesh with its passions and desires. If we live by the Spirit, let us also walk by the Spirit" (Galatians 5:24-25).

The gospel of Christ is what allows us to order the various aspects of our hearts well. This, in turn, empowers us to walk by the Spirit, behaving in ways that bring honor to our Savior. When we choose to believe what God's Word says about our actions, we position ourselves to behave in ways that are as fruitful and delicious as Faye's amazing dessert.

QUESTIONS FOR PERSONAL REFLECTION

1. When it comes to the behavioral ditches outlined in this chapter, do you tend to underemphasize or overemphasize the issue of your behavior?

2. Why does raw behaviorism eventually run out of gas?

3. Why do some people seem to be reluctant to emphasize behaviors in any form or fashion?

QUESTIONS FOR GROUP DISCUSSION

1. Give examples of passages in Scripture that emphasize the kinds of behaviors God desires for his children.

2. What are some examples, from culture, of men and women who are not being held responsible for their behavioral choices?

3. Why and how does the gospel make it easier for us to take responsibility for our actions?

CHAPTER 20

You Are a Speaker

Pastor Cummings, sometimes I think you might just be an angel," Dee remarked.

That drew a hearty guffaw from the pastor. "Sister, I assure you I am very mortal. While I have tried to grow in my relationship with Jesus over the years, I have often failed and still continue to struggle in many ways."

"Wow, I agree with Dee on this one, pastor," said Curt. "I have trouble imagining you sinning."

"Maybe I should just filch that remaining snack off your plate while you're not looking, Curt," the pastor said playfully. "Then you'd believe me."

After the others laughed, Pastor Cummings continued. "Seriously, though, probably the way I have struggled the most over the years, and even continue to struggle now, is with my tongue. Just the other day, I was standing in line at a gas station when an arrogant customer spoke to the female African-American attendant disrespectfully. Before I could catch myself, the anger welled up inside me and I called him a name that was as despicable as many of the hurtful ones I've been called over the years. It was right for me to stand up for the woman, but not in the way I had done so. When I came to my senses, I asked his forgiveness, but the damage was done. I had forgotten what God has said to me in his Word about the power of my tongue."

A POWERFUL CULMINATION OF THE PACKAGE

The true nature of our core beliefs, our chosen thoughts in the moment, our heart's desires, and our emotions are often revealed in the words we choose to speak. The impact of these choices is so significant that King Solomon wrote, "Death and life are in the power of the tongue, and those who love it will eat its fruit" (Proverbs 18:21).

Pause and consider the depth of that metaphor. God is instructing us to believe that our words have the ability to bring death to a situation, relationship, or problem; or conversely, to bring life and healing. Sometimes we become so focused on the wrongdoings of everyone else that we fail to remember God has created us as speakers—men and women who will either bless or curse those the Lord has placed around us. Pastor Cummings's sinful speech at the gas station is a scenario we are all too familiar with. Great damage can be done when we fail to focus on our responsibility to speak carefully and in a manner that pleases Jesus.

EVERY PERSON'S BATTLE

One way the Lord tries to get our attention on this issue is by alerting us to the fact this is a universal problem. Scripture tells us, "We all stumble in many ways. If anyone does not stumble in what he says, he is a perfect man, able to rein in the whole body as well" (James 3:2).

This is one of the reasons we should not spend an inordinate amount of time focusing on the failures of others. We have a sinkhole of potential sin right before our eyes that requires constant attention.

James explained that this war with our tongues can have an incredible impact. He likened our tongues to the rudder of a ship or the bit in a horse's mouth and called on us to recognize that "the tongue is a small part of the body, and yet it boasts of great things" (verse 5). That is what happened with Pastor Cummings at the gas station. One of the smallest parts of his body did a substantial amount of damage.

You would do well to contemplate whether you believe what God's Word says about your communication. Do you factor this into the way you think about your identity so you are better prepared to speak with caution?

Next, James expanded his word pictures to be sure we are convinced about the intensity of this battle we all face:

> See how great a forest is set aflame by such a small fire! And the tongue is a fire, the very world of iniquity; the tongue is set among our members as that which defiles the entire body and sets on fire the course of our life, and is set on fire by hell. For every species of beasts and birds, of reptiles and creatures of the sea, is tamed and has been tamed by the human race. But no one can tame the tongue; it is a restless evil and full of deadly poison (verses 5-8).

No wonder Pastor Cummings laughed when Dee suggested he was an angel incapable of any shortcomings. The Bible paints a very different picture—not just about the pastor, but about you and me as well.

WITH HOPE FOR CHANGE

Because God is a God of grace, he never leaves us in our sin and misery. In Christ, there's always a path to growth in godliness even in this especially challenging area of life. Not surprisingly, the way we speak is prominently highlighted in one of the most important passages on progressive sanctification—Ephesians 4:17-32. After explaining the classic "put off the old man/put on the new man" dynamic in verses 22-24, Paul addressed our communication in several ways to point our hearts and lives in an entirely new direction:

- "Laying aside falsehood, speak truth each one of you with his neighbor, for we are members of one another" (verse 25).

- "Let no unwholesome word proceed from your mouth, but only such a word as is for edification according to the need of the moment, so that it will give grace to those who hear" (verse 29).

- "Be kind to one another, tender-hearted, forgiving each other, just as God in Christ also has forgiven you" (verse 32).

The blood of Christ removes the hopelessness we may feel at times with regard to our speech. No, we will never be perfect in this life, but the Lord also wants us to believe that we can progressively make changes in the way we communicate. We can tell others the truth and do so in ways that edify or build them up. We can learn to speak kindly and do so in ways that are tenderhearted and forgiving. Choose to believe what God says about the power of your words, and ask him to give you the grace to grow in the way you speak.

"CALL 9-1-1!"

Suddenly and without warning, Pastor Cummings grabbed his chest and slumped forward in his chair.

"Grandpa, are you okay?" Walt cried out.

Faye jumped up to grab a wet towel. Andy screamed, "Someone call 9-1-1!"

The next moments were ones the group would never forget.

QUESTIONS FOR PERSONAL REFLECTION

1. What impact does Pastor Cummings's acknowledgment of ongoing struggles with sin have on you?

2. How would you evaluate yourself on the way you use your tongue?

3. Think back over the conversations you have had with others this past week. List examples of when you spoke "words of life" and when you spoke "words of death."

QUESTIONS FOR GROUP DISCUSSION

1. Carefully read James 3 out loud in its entirety. What stands out most to you in this passage, and why?

2. Why is it easier to focus on the shortcomings of others than to pay attention to and believe what God says about the battle we each have with our own tongue?

3. Come up with some examples from God's Word of when people spoke words of death or words or life. Now do the same with examples from contemporary culture.

CHAPTER 21

You Are Prayerful

As the group gathered the following week, there was a sense of heaviness in the air. Everyone had been waiting for an update on Pastor Cummings, but they were apprehensive about what they might hear. Thankfully, the paramedics had arrived quickly, but the medical professionals' demeanor and actions made it obvious that the situation with their beloved pastor was serious.

When Walt walked into the room, he looked ashen and worn. "Grandpa is still in the hospital," he said. "Apparently he has been having heart trouble for some time but kept that news between himself and his doctor because he did not want us to worry."

"Isn't that just like him?" Dee said in between sniffles. "I told you he was an angel."

"The doctors say that the next few weeks are going to be very crucial to his long-term prognosis," Walt said. "Grandpa was fairly alert this morning when I visited him. He said he hated to miss our meeting today because he heard Faye was bringing more pumpkin bars."

Everyone laughed nervously. Even though the situation was somber, they could still imagine the pastor's joyfulness even while he was in the hospital.

"Then he became quiet and reflective and asked me to pass this message along to you," Walt continued. "He said, 'Please ask my friends to pray for me.'"

A PRECIOUS, BLOOD-BOUGHT PRIVILEGE

Trials like the one our group was facing come into our lives in all shapes and sizes practically every day. What you believe about your identity will drive a significant part of your response at such moments. If not considered carefully, life's difficulties can produce some of the garden-variety sins that lurk just below the surface waiting for the next pressure point to reveal their existence. For example, this could be another opportunity for Andy to become angry, or Faye to give in to fear, or Curt to complain, or Walt to worry. Or they could each choose to believe what God has said about them—that they had been created as prayerful beings with direct access to his very throne because of the shed blood of Jesus Christ.

In chapter 10, we looked at how Jesus comforted his disciples in John 14 by telling them that he would send the Holy Spirit, who would indwell them. That passage contains important truths about the power and privilege of prayer. After telling his frightened followers that there was hope for their troubled hearts (John 14:1) and answering both Thomas's and Phillip's objections (verses 5-12), the Lord promised these dear men, "Whatever you ask in My name, that will I do, so that the Father may be glorified in the Son. If you ask Me anything in My name, I will do it" (verses 13-14).

This kind of access to God's throne was secured by Jesus' pending death, burial, and resurrection. Even on the cusp of dying a terrible death, Jesus was focused on the benefits his substitutionary atonement would provide for us.

WITH SUPERNATURAL GUIDANCE

It's in the context of the believer's prayer life that Jesus explains he will ask the Father to send the Spirit to us. Then Jesus makes this stunning affirmation about our identity: "I will not leave you orphans; I will come to you" (verse 18). This is why Paul told the followers of Jesus at Rome that even when we are not sure how to pray, "the Spirit Himself intercedes for us with groanings too deep for words" (Romans 8:26).

This means that Pete, Dee, Curt, Andy, Faye, and Walt are not orphans who must default to sinful reactions when their hearts are broken. They, and we, can be prayerful at such moments because of our position as cherished children in the family of God. We even have God's own Spirit residing in us to help us talk to God directly about our deepest hurts and fears.

Take a moment and consider whether you believe—in a practical sense—what God's Word says about this aspect of your identity. When trials come, do you turn to a sinful response, or do you remind yourself of who you are in Christ and call out to God in prayer for strength and help?

RESULTING IN DIVINE PEACE

Jesus made an additional amazing promise to his disciples: "Peace I leave with you, My peace I give to you; not as the world gives do I give to you. Do not let your heart be troubled, nor let it be fearful" (John 14:27). As we act on our identity as prayerful people, we can be assured of the Spirit's guidance and the Savior's peace.

Years later, Peter would teach this same principle when he said, "[Cast] all your anxiety on Him, because He cares about you" (1 Peter 5:7). Recently, I was discussing this verse with Andrew, our special-needs son. Though he faces a number of mental and physical challenges, he has a way of making biblical truth simple and powerful. He was concerned about an upcoming medical test that day, so I quoted 1 Peter 5:7 and discussed it briefly with him. Andrew thought about the passage for a minute, then said, "Hmmm, that's very nice of him."

I walked away from that conversation with my son about the beauty of prayer and thought, *He's exactly right in his simple yet profound way of viewing God's invitation for us to cast our cares upon him because he cares for us. "Hmmm, that's very nice of him."*

AS AN ANTIDOTE TO ANXIETY

Paul explained this dynamic to his followers in the church at Philippi. Philippians 4:6-7 gives us crucial help in understanding what it means to be prayerful:

> Be anxious for nothing, but in everything by prayer and supplication with thanksgiving let your requests be made known to God. And the peace of God, which surpasses all comprehension, will guard your hearts and your minds in Christ Jesus.

Think back over the past few weeks about occasions when anxiety came into your life. In such moments, is your propensity to pray or not pray? What does that say about the level of your belief in this aspect of who you are in Christ?

SOMETIMES THAT IS ALL YOU CAN DO

The group held hands and cried out to God for their dear pastor. There were plenty of tears and pauses as they expressed their heart-cries to the Lord. They all knew this was not the same group that would have bowed before the Lord just a couple of months earlier. They were no longer defining themselves by their failures and sins. Instead, they knew they were each clothed in the righteousness of Christ. They were children of God, not orphans. They knew the Spirit of God was interceding with and for them. And even in their sorrow, they experienced supernatural peace as they acted on their identity as people who were prayerful.

QUESTIONS FOR PERSONAL REFLECTION

1. How would you evaluate the quality of your prayer life?

2. Have you made wrong evaluations of other aspects of your identity in Christ that are causing prayer to be a less-likely response when trials come?

3. Looking over the past few weeks, list the times when you prayed and the times you could have but didn't. What does this analysis suggest? In what ways can you improve?

QUESTIONS FOR GROUP DISCUSSION

1. What activities and beliefs frequently get in the way of a faithful and vibrant prayer life?

2. How are our spiritual identity in Christ and our prayer lives intertwined?

3. Do you agree or disagree with the following statement? The more biblical a Christian's identity, the more likely that person is to enjoy regular times of prayer with the Lord. Why did you answer the way you did?

CHAPTER 22

You Are Blessed

After the group completed their prayer time, Curt turned to Walt and said, "I find it amazing that your grandpa was able to joke about pumpkin bars even while in the hospital."

"That's a characteristic I noticed each time he joined our studies," Pete said. "He has a quick sense of humor and he often brought joy to our time together. How could a man who faced such injustices throughout his life still maintain such a positive outlook?"

"That's a good question," Walt said. "Now that you mention it, that's one of the primary recollections I have of Grandpa when I was growing up. Yes, he was serious about the things of the Lord, concerned about the racial injustices in our country, and like he told us a few weeks ago, he was far from perfect. But he maintained a level of joy that was infectious. This was true both at home and at church. We even called our worship time on Sundays 'getting happy.'"

"When you think about it," Faye interjected, "Pastor Cummings may have given us a clue to the answer to Pete's question every time he walked into the room."

"What do you mean, Faye?" Andy asked.

"Well, consider the way he always answered each week when we asked him how he was doing."

The group thought for a moment, and their faces lit up almost simultaneously. Together they repeated their pastor's greeting: "Brothers and sisters, I am very blessed."

THE GIVER OF OUR BLESSINGS

One of the reasons we as followers of Christ are able to handle the trials and injustices of life well is because we believe that we are blessed of God. The word *blessed* is not simply a casual or formulaic greeting. To see ourselves as blessed affects the way we think about who we are in Christ.

In his letter to the Ephesian Christians, Paul wrote, "Blessed be the God and Father of our Lord Jesus Christ, who has blessed us with every spiritual blessing in the heavenly places in Christ" (Ephesians 1:3). The word "blessed" is the Greek word *eulogeo*, from which we derive our English word *eulogy*. Paul was inviting these Christians—who had been redeemed out of a thoroughly pagan culture—to contemplate how worthy our God is of adoration and praise. Our blessings find their source in the person and work of our majestic God.

On January 7, 1855, Charles Haddon Spurgeon delivered a sermon on this subject that helps us understand why someone like Pastor Cummings would later feel attached to the importance of being blessed by God. Spurgeon, who was not yet twenty-one years old at the time, said,

> Oh, there is, in contemplating Christ, a balm for every wound, in musing on the Father, there is a quietus for every grief—and in the influence of the Holy Ghost, there is a balsam for every sore. Would you lose your sorrows? Would you drown your cares? Then go plunge yourself in the Godhead's deepest sea; be lost in his immensity; and you shall come forth as from a couch of rest, refreshed and invigorated. I know nothing which can so comfort the soul, so calm the swelling billows of grief and sorrow; so speak peace to the winds of trial, as a devout musing upon the subject of the Godhead.[5]

When Pastor Cummings said that he was blessed, he was thinking first of the nature of his God, who had reached down and redeemed him through the sufficient blood of Jesus Christ. No one could take this reality away from him through any form of discrimination, injustice, or abuse. His identity in Christ shielded his soul even in the midst of the sinful treatment he received in a fallen world.

THE EXTENT OF OUR BLESSINGS

Paul also helped his readers understand that because of their position in Christ, they had been blessed "with every spiritual blessing" (Ephesians 1:3). I grew up in Gary, Indiana, in the early 1960s. This was a turbulent time in our nation's history. Because of the emergence of large steel mills along Lake Michigan, people were moving in from all over the country to take advantage of the good-paying jobs. Gary became a melting pot of people from various ethnicities who were working in very difficult and often unsafe environments.

My mother began taking me and my sisters to the church that was closest to our home at the time, Grace Baptist Church. It was a joyful group of people who had a dramatic impact on my life and future ministry. One of the worship hymns I remember us singing regularly was "Count Your Blessings." I was young at the time and I'm sure the lyrics didn't have the full impact on me that they could have. However, in hindsight, I understand more fully how people living in turbulent times could still possess peace, joy, and purpose. Regardless of what was happening around them, they were focused on all the blessings they possessed in Christ.

THE LOCATION OF OUR BLESSINGS

You may be thinking, *My challenge is that as I look around me, I see many more problems and trials than blessings.* That's why the next part of Paul's statement is so important: Our blessings are found "in the heavenly places" (Ephesians 1:3). Our redemption, hope, forgiveness, calling, adoption, and the many other spiritual blessings Paul lists in Ephesians 1 cannot be touched by the sin-cursed hands or words or motivations of men and women in our fallen culture. These blessings are spiritual realities protected by the power of God.

THE SECURITY OF OUR BLESSINGS

The last two words in Ephesians 1:3 are small, but in many ways they summarize the point of our entire study. Because of your trust in the finished work of Jesus Christ for your salvation, you are now "in Christ."

Pastor Cummings's health problems could not take that away from him. Nor could any other challenge in this life. May his cheerful reply to questions about his well-being be your heart's cry as you face trials and difficulties: "Brothers and sisters, I am very blessed."

QUESTIONS FOR PERSONAL REFLECTION

1. Make a list of your most treasured blessings.

2. Do you tend to focus each day on the blessings you enjoy in Christ or on the frustrations and disappointments you are facing?

3. What adjustments could you make to your daily schedule to begin your day by praising God for your spiritual blessings in Christ? Why do you think starting your day in this way would be beneficial?

QUESTIONS FOR GROUP DISCUSSION

1. Review Ephesians 1 and identify the spiritual blessings Paul enumerates. What other spiritual blessings do we find in other places in God's Word?

2. Why is it often easier to complain about our troubles than focus on this aspect of our identity in Christ?

3. What are some practical ways you can benefit from remembering this aspect of your identity in Christ? In your answers, be sure to include your responses to trials or difficulties.

CHAPTER 23

You Are Growing

As the group prepared to finish this week's session, Pete asked, "How do you think we should structure our meeting next week? Pastor Cummings might not be able to come to lead us."

"That's an interesting question, Pete," Faye said. "The pastor just sort of became our unofficial leader, didn't he?" Everyone nodded and reflected on how much they missed his presence.

"I have an idea," said Dee, "although it might not be very good."

"I think your suggestions are often right on target, Dee," Andy said. "I'd like to hear what you're thinking."

"Maybe the Lord is giving us an opportunity to take another step of growth without Pastor Cummings's guidance," said Dee. "What would happen if each of us came back next week prepared to share another aspect of our identity in Christ that can help us address the areas in which we've struggled most?"

"That's a fabulous idea," said Walt. "But do you think we're ready? That's a pretty big assignment."

"Maybe not two months ago when our group started," said Faye. "But look at us now. We're not the same people. I think Dee's suggested homework will be a great opportunity to show how much we've grown. It will help us to identify the next steps we need to take to continue in the right direction."

"What do you think, everybody?" Pete asked. Each person nodded, although the responsibility of working on the assignment throughout the week and then presenting their results to the entire group was a bit intimidating to them.

"I think you're right, Faye," Walt remarked. "With God's help, we can do this. Great idea, Dee. Thank you for having the courage to share it. I look forward to hearing what everyone has to say next week."

THE HOPE OF PROGRESSIVE SANCTIFICATION

Dee has put her finger on a very important aspect of a believer's identity. Theologians call this *progressive sanctification.* The word *sanctify* means "set apart" or "make holy." Sometimes the Bible uses this term to describe our settled position in Christ, as in 1 Corinthians 6:11. After listing a number of unrighteous conditions that indicated a person would not inherit the kingdom of God, Paul made this stunning affirmation: "Such were some of you; but you were washed, but you were sanctified, but you were justified in the name of the Lord Jesus Christ and in the Spirit of our God." This describes a settled condition in which believers have once and for all been set apart as children of God because of their trust in Christ.

A similar example of positional sanctification is found in Hebrews: "By this will we have been sanctified through the offering of the body of Jesus Christ once for all" (Hebrews 10:10).

God's Word also speaks about sanctification as a process that begins at the moment we trust Christ and continues for the rest of our lives. Jesus prayed for this to occur in us when he asked the Father to "sanctify them in the truth; Your word is truth" (John 17:17). Paul used the term similarly when he spoke to the Ephesians about how Jesus loved the church and gave himself up for her "so that He might sanctify her, having cleansed her by the washing of water with the word" (Ephesians 5:26).

When Dee made her suggestions about the group's homework, she was choosing to believe what God's Word says about them. They were men and women who could, and should, be growing spiritually. Yes, this assignment would be a stretch for them. But that is often the way growth works, which is why the word *progressive* is such an important piece of the puzzle. People who believe this aspect of their identity purposely place themselves in situations where, with the help and enablement of God, they can take the next step of growth.

THE RESOURCES FOR CHRISTIAN GROWTH

Peter focused on this responsibility in his last written words: "Grow in the grace and knowledge of our Lord and Savior Jesus Christ" (2 Peter 3:18). I've always appreciated this passage because of everything else we know about Peter's life. He was far from perfect and his shortcomings were often on vivid display in the Gospels. However, the person who penned 1 and 2 Peter was clearly a changed man. We see in these epistles a humility and depth of character that is refreshingly different than what we saw of the tempestuous fisherman in the Gospels. Yet now at the end of his life and ministry, Peter understood the need for and encouraged believers toward lifelong change and growth.

The fact we can grow in the grace and knowledge of our Lord Jesus Christ should give us tremendous hope. We're not involved in some sort of self-help project where we try to pull ourselves up by our own spiritual bootstraps. We have the knowledge and grace of Jesus Christ at our disposal as we seek to grow in him.

This is why the goal Dee suggested is attainable for each person in their group. Beyond that, it is attainable for you as well. How would you respond to Dee's assignment? What aspect of your identity in Christ should you focus on as you seek to grow to become more like Jesus Christ? How can your Savior's grace and knowledge help you take those next steps with courage?

Please do not be intimidated if you have tried and failed in the past. Let the word *progressive* be your friend. This may be why the Lord recorded so many of Peter's shortcomings in Scripture. A reasonable response to the transformation that took place in Peter could be "If this man could grow, anyone could." Perhaps this is why Peter ended his epistle the way he did—because he could wholeheartedly agree with that analysis.

THE GOAL OF SANCTIFICATION

Peter concluded his second epistle with a beautiful doxology that fuels and directs our attempts to grow spiritually: "To Him be the glory, both now and to the day of eternity" (2 Peter 3:18). If each person in the group takes Dee's challenge seriously, then Christ will be glorified.

That is what is at stake in our lives as well. That is why it's important for us to choose to believe what God has said about the possibility that we can grow in sanctification. We honor the Lord when we take steps in the direction Peter has outlined for us: "Grow in the grace and knowledge of our Lord and Savior Jesus Christ" (2 Peter 3:18).

QUESTIONS FOR PERSONAL REFLECTION

1. What evidence is there in your life that you believe what God says about the possibility and responsibility of spiritual growth?

2. Consider the emphases in our culture, and perhaps even in your own life, that suggest human beings cannot change. Where and how does this wrong message emerge?

3. Do you know any "contemporary Peters" whose lives demonstrate how God has enabled them to take clear and observable steps toward progressive sanctification?

QUESTIONS FOR GROUP DISCUSSION

1. Are you ready to take on the same challenge Dee issued to her friends? (If you're in a group, take turns answering this.)

2. What characteristics will help facilitate Christian growth in your life, and what characteristics will hinder such growth?

3. What are some books and other resources you have found helpful in your journey toward progressive sanctification?

CHAPTER 24

You Are a Lamb

As everyone returns after a week of study and reflection, there's a sense of anticipation in the air. After opening in prayer for their time together, Pete asked, "How did everyone do on your assignment? Did you find it harder or easier than you expected?"

Curt spoke up first. "It's been a long time since I had to do homework. But when I sat down at the kitchen table one evening with my Bible and the notes from our previous sessions, something surprising happened."

"Tell us about it," said Faye. "I wonder if we all had a similar experience?"

"Well," Curt continued, "at first I thought I wouldn't be able to come up with any additional aspects of my identity in Christ that could help guide my next steps. But after I reviewed the twenty-plus truths we've already discussed, I started thinking of other ways that God's Word describes us that we haven't talked about yet. Before long, I had a list of many other word pictures from Scripture. It took me a while to narrow my list down to only one to share."

"That's interesting," Pete said. "It was harder for me, although maybe I should have started earlier in the week. But you're right, Curt. After a while, I had several ideas to choose from."

"I really struggled," said Andy. "Even though our previous sessions together have been helpful and interesting, thinking this way about who I am in Jesus is still stretching me. I eventually came up with an answer, but it wasn't easy. That's what I like about being part of this group. I'm looking forward to hearing what everybody else has to say. I think this process will come easier to me after I hear your answers."

"Who would like to go first?" Walt asked. Everyone looked around and smiled because by now they knew each other well enough to see the humor in their nervousness. Plus, they had an immediate opportunity to apply what they had been studying all these weeks together. Would they define themselves according to their old ways of thinking, or by believing what God's Word says about them?

"I'll try," Pete volunteered. "Although I think the one I chose might make you laugh." He paused and swallowed hard. "I think it's important for me to believe that God says that I am a lamb. An important part of my identity is how I am dependent on the provision of my great Shepherd."

"That answer doesn't make me laugh, but it is surprising," said Dee. "Why do you think that particular illustration came to your mind?"

"So much of my life has been focused on my accomplishments, my strength, my abilities, and my resources," Pete said. "This week I meditated on a Bible passage that I learned as a little boy, Psalm 23. I memorized much of it in Sunday school, but it has been a long time since I've truly thought about what it means for the Lord to be my shepherd and me to be one of his lambs. I want to crucify my pride by living more in dependence on his strength and less on my own."

THE LORD IS YOUR SHEPHERD

Our church has an annual outreach activity known as the Lafayette Living Nativity. The program features fourteen scenes depicting various aspects of the Christmas story, beginning at the Garden of Eden and culminating at the second coming of Christ. Live camels, donkeys, and sheep are included along with hundreds of costumed actors from our church family.

My son, Andrew, and I have spent many years dressed as shepherds in the "Journey to Bethlehem" scene. Because Andrew is blind, I have to carefully lead him out to the set and place him in the proper position so the passing cars can watch us as we stand in the middle of a flock of sheep and point to the star of Bethlehem, which stands above the roof of the church. I have always experienced a fascinating mixture of emotions as I have contemplated my son's dependence on me and thought about Jesus' willingness to become the perfect Lamb of God so that we, in turn, could trust his work on the cross and live in dependence on him as our great Shepherd. The convergence of biblical images in my mind and heart is delightful and delicious.

Lambs are fascinating creatures. Andrew spends the entire evening holding the back of one of the sheep for stability and shouting out, "Say bah, sheep." And right on cue, over and over, the sheep all say, "Bah." You should hear Andrew laugh every time the sheep obey him. There is a simplicity and beauty to their design and function that is joyful to behold.

AN ANTIDOTE TO OUR PRIDE

Believing this aspect of our identity—that we are lambs—can help us remember how much we need the provision and sustenance of our great Shepherd. Every line of Psalm 23 reminds us of this blessed reality. If you have not memorized this passage, I would encourage you to do so. Choosing to believe that "the LORD is my Shepherd" (Psalm 23:1) is both comforting and challenging, along with all the other truths we read in the text.

As a pastor, I think back on the numerous gravesites where I have quoted this psalm to grieving family members and friends. The immediate impact is palpable as God's children are reminded of their identity as lambs of God and the strength we can find in our loving Shepherd.

Isaiah is one of the many authors of Scripture, humanly speaking, who used this word picture to help God's people adopt a correct understanding of their identity. His audience, primarily the tribe of Judah in the 700s BC, was facing the judgment of God in part because of their proud idolatry and rejection of the Lord. Early in the book he affirmed,

"The pride of man will be humbled, and the loftiness of men will be abased; and the LORD alone will be exalted in that day, but the idols will completely vanish" (Isaiah 2:17-18).

Thankfully, the prophecy does not end there. A marvelous transition occurs in Isaiah 40:1 as Isaiah contemplates a day when, because of the redemptive work of the promised Messiah (Isaiah 53), God's people will replace their pride with humility and dependence. Isaiah said that in that day, "Like a shepherd He will tend His flock, in His arm He will gather the lambs and carry them in His bosom; He will gently lead the nursing ewes" (Isaiah 40:11).

Ultimately this word picture points to the cross of Christ, which makes this kind of transformation possible. When we choose to think about ourselves as lambs, we are identifying with Christ's death, burial, and resurrection. As Peter reminded his readers, we are redeemed "with precious blood, as of a lamb unblemished and spotless, the blood of Christ" (1 Peter 1:19).

The group sat quietly and contemplated what Pete had shared. His answer was not only a surprise, it evidenced an important step of growth. They knew their friend was on his way to conquering pride in his heart and life as he chose to believe what God's Word said about his identity in Christ.

QUESTIONS FOR PERSONAL REFLECTION

1. When is the last time you thought about yourself as a lamb? Why do you think the Lord would want you to think about yourself in that way?

2. What does it mean for God to be your great Shepherd? How should this impact your daily thoughts, desires, words, and choices?

3. How can this aspect of your identity help you when you struggle with pride?

QUESTIONS FOR GROUP DISCUSSION

1. Pete selected an aspect of his identity with Christ that was unexpected. Do you think there is wisdom in Christians choosing to meditate on biblical word pictures that are opposite of the ways they sometimes function when behaving sinfully? Why?

2. Discuss specific life situations that would be affected by believing the truth that we are lambs of God.

3. Describe people who believe, using the language of Isaiah 40:11, they are being tended by the great Shepherd and carried in his bosom.

CHAPTER 25

You Are an Ambassador

Y ou know, Pete," Curt shared, "at first I agreed with Dee when she said your choice to focus on being a lamb with a great Shepherd was surprising. But after you explained your reasoning, I thought to myself, *That's quite powerful.*"

"I would have never thought of that concept either, Pete," said Walt. "But thanks for sharing it with us. Now I can think of many ways that will impact me as well."

"Who would like to go next?" Faye asked.

"I'll try," Curt said. "The one that really stood out to me is that I need to believe how God has said I'm his ambassador."

As everyone thought for a moment about Curt's answer, Andy spoke up. "That one is almost as surprising as Pete's. I don't think that would have ever come to my mind. Why did it rise to the top for you, Curt?"

"Well, you know I've struggled with complaining," Curt reflected. "I'm sure I was hard to listen to during our first weeks together." There was an awkward silence, then everyone broke out laughing.

"We all brought a lot of baggage and bad habits into our group," said Faye. "It has been fun to watch God change us."

"As I was working on the assignment last week," Curt continued, "It struck me how often my words were representing my opinions, desires, and even my hurts and disappointments. It was all about me. I didn't think about all the missed opportunities to represent and speak on behalf of my King."

"That's rich, Curt," Walt said. "Was there anything in particular that we've been studying together that helped you start turning the corner in your thinking?"

"It goes back to an observation Andy made several weeks ago," Curt answered.

Curt's words caught Andy's attention. "Why do I have the same feeling in the pit of my stomach like I used to have in grade school when I was about to get in trouble in class?" Andy asked.

Curt laughed. "No, really. It was the day you talked about our union with Christ. So much of my life has been lived for me, myself, and I. Only recently have I realized I need to believe what God says about my identity. The more I considered that Christ was in me, and I was in him, the more I wanted my words to represent his perspective on my situation. I truly want to be his ambassador."

"That also says something about you too, Andy," Walt suggested.

"What do you mean?" Andy asked.

"You've told us several times that you feel like you're just an uneducated factory worker," Walt said. "But your insights have been a blessing to all of us. And what you just suggested is solid gold, Curt. How cool is it that we can be ambassadors of Christ!"

BECAUSE ALL THINGS HAVE BECOME NEW

In 2 Corinthians 5, we find a treasure trove of information about our identity in Christ. There, Paul told the immature but growing believers in Corinth that he didn't view them through the lens of external standards because the most important aspects of their identity involved internal spiritual realities. That was his point when he said, "From now on we recognize no one according to the flesh" (verse 16). He then affirmed, "Therefore if anyone is in Christ, he is a new creature; the old things passed away; behold, new things have come" (verse 17).

This is why someone like Curt does not have to remain stuck in his habits of complaining until the day God takes him home. He can change because he is a "new creature" who is now "in Christ." The same is true for you and me. We can and must believe what God says about the new potential we possess because of what Christ has done and continues to do on our behalf.

BECAUSE WE VALUE RECONCILIATION

The story does not end at our salvation. Amazingly, now that we are united with Jesus, God has given us the ministry of reconciliation. Paul wrote, "Now all these things are from God, who reconciled us to Himself through Christ and gave us the ministry of reconciliation" (2 Corinthians 5:18). This is why complaining, or any kind of sinful speech, is so unbecoming for a follower of the Lord. In such moments, we are failing to believe what God's Word says about us.

Conversely, when we choose to process our hurts and difficulties through the lens of the gospel, we can then live and speak in a way that potentially reconciles someone else to Jesus. Recently our church family heard the testimony of a man who came to our counseling ministry after struggling for years with drug and alcohol addiction. His body is scarred with the evidence of his sin. His wife and children have paid a significant price for this man's past choices. However, by God's grace, he repented of his sin and placed his faith in Christ. He has a long way to go and everyone involved in his story knows that. Still, the change has already been demonstrable and is living proof of the truth of Paul's words in 2 Corinthians 5. In his testimony, this man invited others to trust Christ for the forgiveness of their sins. In doing this, he was believing that God had committed to him the ministry of reconciliation.

PLEADING WITH THOSE AROUND US

That we are ambassadors for Christ is a major aspect of our identity in him. There truly is a heaven to be gained and a hell to be shunned.

Therefore, God calls us to believe that "we are ambassadors for Christ, as though God were making an appeal through us; we beg you on behalf of Christ, be reconciled to God" (2 Corinthians 5:20). In so doing, we are cooperating with the work of our Savior as explained in the previous verse: "that God was in Christ reconciling the world to Himself, not counting their trespasses against them" (verse 19).

That means that when we're thinking properly about our identity, we won't have time for wasteful words of complaining, bickering, or judging. We have a far more important calling and a much more exciting mission. God has called us to be his ambassadors, representing him in each moment of our lives in a way that can have eternal impact on the people he has placed around us.

BECAUSE OF THE POWER OF THE GOSPEL

When we consider all our shortcomings and sins, many of us struggle with believing that God could use us in this way. Keep in mind that the recipients of these instructions were far from perfect—the Corinthian church was perhaps the most immature of any of the churches Paul addressed. Yet ultimately, these principles are true not because of who we are, but whose righteousness we are wearing. This is why Paul concluded 2 Corinthians 5 with this affirmation: "He made Him who knew no sin to be sin on our behalf, so that we might become the righteousness of God in Him" (verse 21). The imputed righteousness of Christ and his resurrection power working within us makes it possible for us to represent him well.

QUESTIONS FOR PERSONAL REFLECTION

1. Do you struggle with complaining or other forms of speech that displease God? How can and should the concept of being an ambassador of Christ impact your choices each day?

2. When is the last time you spoke to someone about becoming a follower of Jesus? What holds you back from being more faithful in this calling?

3. What ambassador of Christ did the Lord use to draw you to himself? What barriers and fears did that person have to overcome before speaking to you?

QUESTIONS FOR GROUP DISCUSSION

1. Make a list of faithful ambassadors for Christ in God's Word. What characteristics did they have in common? What do you think motivated them to believe this aspect of what God says about his children?

2. Make a list of faithful ambassadors for Christ in your spheres of influence. What characteristics do they have in common? What do you think motivates them to believe this aspect of what God says about his children?

3. Ask others in your group to hold you accountable for believing and functioning as an ambassador of Christ. Review Ephesians 6:18-20, then spend time praying as a group that God would give you the boldness to speak words of reconciliation to those the Lord has placed around you. (If you're not part of a group, consider asking a trusted Christian friend to hold you accountable.)

CHAPTER 26

You Are Victorious

I wish Pastor Cummings was here so he could have heard what Pete and Curt just shared," said Faye. "I can see him smiling and saying, 'Great job, my dear friends, great job!'"

"That's so true," said Dee. Turning to Walt, she asked, "Can you give us an update on your grandpa's condition?"

"Thank you for your prayers, everyone," said Walt. "He's stable, but honestly, the doctors say his days on earth are coming to an end." Upon hearing this, the group became silent. This news wasn't unexpected, but it was still hard to face.

"Can we stop and pray for him now?" Curt asked.

Dee began, and everyone took turns praying for their beloved pastor. There were tears as they asked the Lord to draw Pastor Cummings close to himself and to give Walt and every family member, church member, and friend sustaining grace.

"I visited Grandpa this morning in the hospital, and at first, I wasn't going to attend our group meeting today," Walt said. "But he encouraged me to come after he and I talked about the homework we gave each other last week. Then he gave me a message for each of you, but told me I should not share it until after he passed." That news intrigued everybody, and they silently wondered what the pastor's final wishes for them might be.

"I asked Grandpa how he thought I should complete my assignment for today, especially in light of the way I tend to worry," said Walt. "I have been that way since I was a little boy, and Grandpa knows that all too well. Then he squeezed my hand tightly and said, 'Son, you need to believe what God says about how, in Jesus, you are victorious.'"

BECAUSE GOD KEEPS HIS COVENANTS

As we learned in the previous chapter, as believers, we are united with Jesus. One of the many blessings of being united with him is that as we pursue his purposes, we are guaranteed supernatural blessing and ultimate victory. Scripture is filled with affirmations of this reassuring truth.

For example, after Genesis 1–11 presents the four key events of creation, the fall, the flood, and the tower of Babel, readers are left wondering if there is any hope for sin-cursed mankind. The answer is found in Genesis 12:1-3, where God comes to a man named Abram (later renamed Abraham) and makes an important and eternal covenant with him:

> The LORD said to Abram, "Go forth from your country, and from your relatives and from your father's house, to the land which I will show you; and I will make you a great nation, and I will bless you, and make your name great; and so you shall be a blessing; and I will bless those who bless you, and the one who curses you I will curse. And in you all the families of the earth will be blessed" (Genesis 12:1-3).

These verses become the skeleton on which the story of God's redemption in Christ hangs. Consider how much God was calling Abram to believe about himself in that passage. Thankfully, a few chapters later, we read that Abram "believed in the LORD; and He reckoned it to him as righteousness" (Genesis 15:6). This concept is so central to what it means to have a relationship with God that the apostle Paul quoted these same words in Romans 4:3 as he discussed the primacy of believing what God says about us.

Note that God promised to bless Abram and that through him, the families of the earth would be blessed. Abram would experience victory so that others could understand the power and majesty of God.

REGARDLESS OF THE
NUMBER OF OPPOSING KINGS

It did not take long for this promise to begin to find fulfillment. Genesis 14 records the amazing battle of the kings. If you have never studied it before, I encourage you to do so, although you might need a Bible atlas to keep all the names and places clear in your mind. However, that is the point. When a coalition of four kings beats another coalition of five kings and inadvertently sweeps Abram's nephew Lot and his family up in the plunder, Abram rallies a group of 318 men and chases after them. In one of the more understated verses in the entire Bible, we read, "He divided his forces against them by night, he and his servants, and defeated them, and pursued them as far as Hobah, which is north of Damascus" (Genesis 14:15).

Did you see that? God allowed this patriarch and his relatively small band of men to defeat a coalition of powerful Mesopotamian kings.

AS AN OPPORTUNITY TO MAGNIFY
HIS POWERFUL NAME THROUGH YOU

The next verses explain the reason for Abram's victory. Out of nowhere, a mysterious priest-king named Melchizedek appears and in front of the wicked, defeated king of Sodom says, "Blessed be Abram of God Most High, possessor of heaven and earth; and blessed be God Most High, who has delivered your enemies into your hand" (Genesis 14:19-20).

We find stories like this throughout the Bible because the Lord wants us to believe that in him, we can be victorious. This is why King David, just before his death, reminded the people, "Yours, O Lord, is the greatness and the power and the glory and the victory and the majesty, indeed everything that is in the heavens and the earth; Yours is the dominion, O Lord, and You exalt Yourself as head over all" (1 Chronicles 29:11).

When people like Walt, you, and me choose to worry, it is because we are focusing on our own resources instead of the strength available to us from our heavenly Father. He wants us to choose to believe that in him, we can have victory.

A THEME OF HOPE FOR GOD'S PEOPLE

One of the last recorded prophets in the Old Testament emphasized this principle to encourage God's people to look forward to a time when the promised Messiah would guarantee their victory. He concluded his book with this prediction:

> In that day it will be said to Jerusalem: "Do not be afraid, O Zion; do not let your hands fall limp. The Lord your God is in your midst, a victorious warrior. He will exult over you with joy, He will be quiet in His love, He will rejoice over you with shouts of joy" (Zephaniah 3:16-17).

When Jesus walked the earth, he began demonstrating to people the victory available in him, especially for those who were beaten down and oppressed. Matthew explained to his readers that this was to fulfill Isaiah's prophecy:

> Behold, My Servant whom I have chosen; My Beloved in whom My soul is well-pleased; I will put My Spirit upon Him, and He shall proclaim justice to the Gentiles. He will not quarrel, nor cry out; nor will anyone hear His voice in the streets. A battered reed He will not break off, and a smoldering wick He will not put out, Until He leads justice to victory. And in His name the Gentiles will hope" (Matthew 12:18-21).

Don't you love that promise—that Jesus Christ will lead justice to victory? This is why someone like Pastor Cummings could experience terrible injustice in this life yet still cling to the hope of ultimate victory in Jesus. Abraham's faith was Pastor Cummings's faith as well (see Romans 4:13–5:5). The march to victorious justice in this life is slow and uncertain. Still, "having been justified by faith, we have peace with God through our Lord Jesus Christ, through whom also we have obtained our introduction by faith into this grace in which we stand; and we exult in hope of the glory of God" (Romans 5:1-2). God's people can defeat worry by believing what he says about their final victory in and through him.

QUESTIONS FOR PERSONAL REFLECTION

1. What other verses come to your mind when you think about the victories God gives his people?

2. What hymns or Christian songs come to mind about the victories that are ours in Christ?

3. How would your daily life be different if you more regularly contemplated your victory in Christ?

QUESTIONS FOR GROUP DISCUSSION

1. Review Genesis 14 and try to sort out the various kings involved in this epic battle. Why was this victory so amazing from a human perspective?

2. Share the story of someone in your life who lives in light of their promised victory in Christ. How does this person's example impact you?

3. Read 1 Corinthians 15 and contemplate how the resurrection of Jesus Christ secures our victory over even death itself. What do you find most encouraging about this?

CHAPTER 27

You Are Hopeful

W ell, Dee," Faye remarked, "the gentlemen have done really well so far. But now I think it's the ladies' turn, don't you?"

"I think you're right, Faye," said Dee, "although what Pete, Curt, and Walt have shared has set the bar high and I'm also looking forward to what Andy has to say. Hearing about the ways each of you are growing spiritually is amazing."

"I've come to realize the Lord wants me to believe that I am the recipient of great hope," Dee said. "My husband and I took some time this week to study what the Bible says about hope. He found a concordance that lists the use of every word in the Bible, and we were amazed how often the Lord tells us we can find our hope in him regardless of the circumstance we're facing."

"Why do you think that concept was so powerful to you?" Andy asked.

Dee thought for a moment. "I'm ashamed to admit that so often I use phrases like 'you're hopeless' or 'that's hopeless' in the way I speak to myself and others. You guys are my friends and I know I can trust you, so I'll just lay it out there. In the morning, I would often look in the mirror and think about all my failures and remind myself how hopeless I am. I have been in the habit of telling my husband, when he fails me, that there is no hope for him or our marriage. It breaks my heart that I even found myself saying such words to our toddler a few weeks back when he broke a glass figurine my mother gave me."

A bit tearful, Dee paused, then continued: "But I realize those words are lies. Lies from the father of lies himself, which just drove me further into despair and depression. Walt, this goes along with what you were just saying from Romans chapters 4 and 5 about being victorious. In Christ, I have reason for great hope now and in the days ahead. If God doesn't view me as hopeless, then neither should I. I want to learn what it means to believe what God says about the hope I have in Jesus."

WE REJOICE IN HOPE

Dee is right that Romans 5 mentions a number of reasons to believe that we are the recipients of great hope. Paul goes so far to exclaim that "we exult in hope of the glory of God" (verse 2). This is an amazing statement in light of all that Paul wrote earlier in Romans about our depravity and utter inability to save ourselves.

And that is not the end of the story for those who choose to repent of their sin and place their faith in Christ. Romans 5:1 tells us, "Having been justified by faith, we have peace with God through our Lord Jesus Christ." We have been declared righteous by our holy God because our sin is forgiven, and we are clothed in the righteousness of our Savior.

It is a terrible lie to ever look in the mirror and announce that we are hopeless. God says otherwise, and he instructs us to believe his analysis of our position in Christ. Through our Lord Jesus Christ, "we have obtained our introduction by faith into this grace in which we stand" (verse 2). These are the kinds of truths God calls us to believe each day. It's not a matter of thinking more highly of ourselves, but of thinking more highly of the work of grace that God has done and continues to do in our lives for his glory and our good.

EVEN WHILE SUFFERING

Paul then said that this hope is so powerful that it can help us withstand all the trials of life. "Not only this, but we also exult in our tribulations" (verse 3). All of us experience times when we are often tempted to give up and pronounce the verdict of hopeless on ourselves and those around us. How is it possible for us to rejoice in hope during a time of tribulation?

Paul anticipated that question and answered it comprehensively: "We also exult in our tribulations, knowing that tribulation brings about perseverance; and perseverance, proven character; and proven character, hope" (verses 3-4). Hope can be found in the fact that God is working in and refining us as we endure trials and disappointments. The situations we are tempted to say are hopeless are often actually the polar opposite. Our hope is not in immediate relief or reliance upon our own strength, but in the final outcome, which is greater Christlikeness as we walk with him through the fiery trials that test our faith.

HOPE THAT WILL NOT DISAPPOINT

Paul concluded this passage with these amazing words: "Hope does not disappoint, because the love of God has been poured out within our hearts through the Holy Spirit who was given to us" (verse 5). No wonder Paul began this book by affirming that he was not ashamed of the gospel (Romans 1:16). Where else could people like you and me find hope that was guaranteed not to disappoint? If God's love has been poured out to us through the Spirit, we can rest assured that there is hope for growth and redemption every day regardless of the challenges we might face.

Christians who choose to believe what God says about their reasons for hope develop a joyful, faithful outlook that is infectious. Don't let hopelessness rob you of the confidence and strength the Lord offers you each day. You have his word on it—his hope will not disappoint.

QUESTIONS FOR PERSONAL REFLECTION

1. Do you ever use the word *hopeless* to describe yourself or those around you? In what circumstances do you typically arrive at that conclusion?

2. What is the relationship between the gospel and a believer's hope?

3. How is Paul's argument in Romans 5:1-5 different than the world's "power of positive thinking"?

QUESTIONS FOR GROUP DISCUSSION

1. Give some examples of people in the Bible whose lives evidenced hope that did not disappoint.

2. Give some examples of people you know who have learned to rejoice in hope. What kind of impact do they have on you and others?

3. Trace Paul's argument in Romans 5:3-4. Specifically, how can tribulation bring about perseverance, and perseverance bring about proven character?

CHAPTER 28

You Are a Soldier

Dee, that was fantastic!" said Faye. "I'm so glad you felt comfortable enough to open up to us about ways you have struggled."

"It's not easy," Dee confessed. "I have never been part of a group like this. But now I understand why God has created his church to be a body of brothers and sisters growing in Christ together. Having people like you in my life who I can be honest with is a new experience—one for which I am profoundly thankful."

Everyone nodded as they contemplated what Dee shared. Andy spoke next: "There are several responses rumbling around my mind. First, every one of the answers each of you has given so far is much different than I would have expected. However, as soon as you shared your reasoning, I could see why the Lord directed you in that way. Second, what God taught each of you is helpful to me. I, too, am a lamb with a great Shepherd, an ambassador of Christ, victorious, and a recipient of great hope. I agree with you, Dee—being in a group like this has been life-changing.

"Third," Andy continued, "is that your answers also impact the way I think about you, as well as other followers of Jesus I know. It's not just a matter of choosing to believe what God says about me, but also what he says about the men and women around me."

"That's so true, Andy," said Faye. Taking a deep breath, she continued,

"Would anyone like to guess the aspect of our identity that came to my mind?"

"No way," Pete said. "Not after being surprised four times in a row now. I think this exercise also shows how rich the Word of God is. No wonder the apostle Peter said it was all we need for life and godliness."[6]

"I'm tempted to make a few clucking sounds and call you chickens," Faye said jokingly. "But I feel the same way because we still haven't heard Andy's answer and I have no idea what he's about to say. But for me, I want to do a better job of remembering that I am a soldier."

Silence. Sweet Faye. All five feet two inches of her. Barely 100 pounds with graying hair. A soldier?

Finally, Curt had the courage to ask what was on everyone else's mind. "Faye, we're going to need some help with that one. Why did you pick that it is important for you to believe that God says you are a soldier?"

Faye chuckled. "Are you having trouble picturing me in full military attire? I have often allowed fear to consume my heart, and in response, I have tried to insulate myself from problems in my own strength. It dawned on me this week that I am a soldier of Christ and that ultimately, the battle belongs to the Lord."

A REGULAR EMPHASIS IN THE OLD TESTAMENT

As God began to fulfill his covenants to the children of Abraham, the young nation was often involved in literal battles with the kings and countries around them. And it was apparent from the beginning that the Lord was calling them to view their responsibility in a unique way. King Solomon observed that "the horse is prepared for the day of battle, but victory belongs to the LORD" (Proverbs 21:31).

Solomon certainly had many opportunities to learn that lesson from the exploits of his father, David. Do you remember what the sweet singer of Israel said to Goliath before slaying him with a simple stone and sling?

You come to me with a sword, a spear, and a javelin, but I come to you in the name of the LORD of hosts, the God of the armies of Israel, whom you have taunted. This day the LORD will deliver you up into my hands, and I will strike you down and remove your head from you. And I will give the dead bodies of the army of the Philistines this day to the birds of the sky and the wild beasts of the earth, that all the earth may know that there is a God in Israel, and that all this assembly may know that the LORD does not deliver by sword or by spear; for the battle is the LORD's and He will give you into our hands (1 Samuel 17:45-47).

Soldiers in God's army were able to face battles with supernatural courage and strength because ultimately it was God who was fighting on their behalf.

USED TO DESCRIBE SOME OF GOD'S CHOICE SERVANTS

The New Testament expands the soldier metaphor to include all men and women who perform God's will and work. For example, Paul reminded Timothy to "suffer hardship with me, as a good soldier of Christ Jesus" (2 Timothy 2:3). He certainly was not instructing his son in the faith to secure a sword or spear and use military methods to accomplish the purpose of the church. But he did want this young pastor to add this word picture to his list of ways he thought about himself. Timothy could overcome his fear and timidity by choosing to believe what God said about who he was in Christ.

Another example is the way Paul described a man named Epaphroditus. This was the person—perhaps one of their pastors—whom the Philippian church had trusted to deliver their love offering to Paul in prison. Unfortunately, Epaphroditus became seriously ill on the journey. This news concerned the Christians in Philippi, which, in turn, troubled Epaphroditus because he didn't want the church to worry about him. In describing this faithful man, Paul said, "I thought it necessary to send to you Epaphroditus, my brother and fellow worker and fellow soldier, who is also your messenger and minister to my need" (Philippians 2:25). He went on to say, "Receive him then in the Lord with all joy, and hold men like him in high regard; because he came close to death for the work of Christ, risking his life to complete what was deficient in your service to me" (verses 29-30).

Paul thought of this faithful man in many ways, including the fact he was a fellow soldier in Christ. You and I can address our fears and worries by thinking about ourselves in the same way. Why would we ever be afraid if we truly believed the Lord is fighting on our behalf?

IT IS TIME TO FIND YOUR ARMOR

Perhaps the quintessential passage in God's Word on this subject is Ephesians 6:10-20, where Paul instructs us to "take up the full armor of God, so that you will be able to resist in the evil day, and having done everything, to stand firm" (verse 13). Verse after verse describes specific aspects of the armor God provides for us as we fight against our adversary as good soldiers of Jesus Christ.

Maybe we underestimated Faye after all, and until now, she evidently underestimated herself. She is not simply an elderly woman, small of stature, having to face the challenges of aging by herself. She needs to believe that she is a soldier of Jesus Christ, and that she can move forward with courage and hope. Our God always promises to go before us because, in the final analysis, the battle belongs to the Lord.

QUESTIONS FOR PERSONAL REFLECTION

1. What evidence is there in your life that you believe you are a soldier of Christ?

2. Do you believe that in your case, ultimately the battle belongs to the Lord? Do you tend to live life in his power and strength, or your own? In what ways can you improve in this area?

3. Reflect on the story of David and Goliath in 1 Samuel 17. How does this seminal event in the history of Israel demonstrate the importance of believing what God says about who we are?

QUESTIONS FOR GROUP DISCUSSION

1. Read Ephesians 6:10-20. What are the various aspects of the armor of God, and how do they apply to the way we think about ourselves today?

2. What is the difference between fighting in the Lord's strength and being an antagonistic person who engages in needless warfare?

3. Who do you know that lives as a good soldier of Jesus Christ? What does that woman or man do, or not do, that would cause you to view them as a soldier?

CHAPTER 29

You Are a Student

Okay, now I'm batting 0 for 5," said Andy. "I would have never guessed any of the answers each of you have given. But they were all great. Anyone want to take a stab at the one that came to my mind?"

Everyone playfully shook their heads. Pete continued, "This exercise is showing the depth and riches of the Bible. I'm getting the feeling that we're just scratching the surface of all the ways God describes us in his Word."

"And doesn't that prove just how much he loves us?" said Walt. "We all have different backgrounds and struggles, along with unique ways to process information. And God has given us a book that is filled with variety. Each concept we have studied about our identity in Christ has the ability to adjust the way we think about ourselves and those the Lord has placed around us."

"That's so true," said Dee. "And when you add the fact that the Lord has given us his Spirit to guide us as we try to understand and apply Scripture to our hearts and lives, that is a powerful combination."

"Okay, Andy, we can't wait any longer," Pete said.

"Well, here goes," Andy replied. "I want to do a better job of remembering that God has called me to be a student."

Walt raised his eyebrows. "Can you unpack that one for us. Andy? I think that makes our sixth surprise in a row."

"I've spoken a lot about my anger problem the past couple of months," Andy continued. "It hasn't been easy for me to do that because I am ashamed of the way I've behaved. I mean, I go to church every Sunday and say I'm a Christian, and then I explode at work or home when things aren't going my way. It dawned on me the other day that my anger is frequently just a lazy person's way of dealing with frustration. I've hidden behind the excuse that I barely made it through high school, so I'm not as smart as other people. But the real issue is that I haven't wanted to carefully examine what is happening in my heart when I'm angry. God instructs me to study his Word and learn from him. In the future, I want to be a more careful and diligent student."

GOD MADE YOU WITH THIS CAPACITY

The psalmist affirmed of God, "Your hands made me and fashioned me; give me understanding, that I may learn Your commandments" (Psalm 119:73). In this beautiful psalm about the glory and sufficiency of God's Word, the writer makes the logical connection between being made in the image of God and possessing the ability to learn and apply what Scripture teaches. Andy is right to view himself as a student in the very best sense of that word. God created his mind to think carefully, even when frustrated or disappointed about what is occurring. This is why the psalmist explained two verses earlier, "It is good for me that I was afflicted, that I may learn your statutes."

Recently I had the privilege of concluding a counseling case with a couple from our community who had come seeking help for their marriage. They both struggled mightily with anger, albeit in very different ways. However, they were tired of where their sinful approaches had taken them, and they truly wanted to learn a different path.

And that is exactly what happened. They dug into their Bibles week after week and learned what God's Word says about how to process trials. They chose to believe that God calls them— and all of his children—to be students. By God's grace, they were faithful and effective learners.

ON THE PATH TO WISDOM

It was easy for Andy to hide behind the excuse "I'm just a factory worker with limited knowledge." The truth is, he possesses more education than many of the original recipients of God's Word. Still, the Lord calls his people to be careful students so they can grow in biblical wisdom. For example:

- "A wise man will hear and increase in learning, and a man of understanding will acquire wise counsel" (Proverbs 1:5).

- "Give instruction to a wise man and he will be still wiser, teach a righteous man and he will increase his learning" (Proverbs 9:9).

Andy was also right in concluding that his sinful explosions were "the lazy man's" way of responding to situations he did not like. It takes effort and conviction to slow down and examine our hearts before speaking and acting. But that is exactly what faithful students do, in the power and wisdom of the Holy Spirit of God.

WITH A GENTLE INVITATION

Some of my favorite church members are women and men who are lifelong learners. Many are older than me and have been followers of Jesus Christ decades longer than I have. Yet they come to church each Lord's day with a hunger and thirst to study God's Word. As I have gotten to know these dear brothers and sisters over the years, I have discovered that a common thread for many of them is their belief that being a student is a privileged position in response to this gentle invitation from their Savior:

Come to Me, all who are weary and heavy-laden, and I will give you rest. Take My yoke upon you and learn from Me, for I am gentle and humble in heart, and you will find rest for your souls (Matthew 11:28-29).

Jesus Christ himself invites us to learn from him. Wise people marvel at that invitation and choose to believe that God has called them to be his students.

THEN THE PHONE RANG

Just as Andy was finishing, Walt's cell phone sounded. "Oh no," he said as he stood up abruptly and began to exit the room. "It's from the hospital. Excuse me, but I better take this."

Everyone looked at one another fearing the worst. Instinctively, they bowed their heads and took turns praying for Pastor Cummings and those who were caring for him.

After they had all prayed, Walt returned. Obviously shaken, he reached down to gather his things. "I can't believe it," Walt said. "I knew this day could come, but I didn't think it would be today. The nurse just told me that Grandpa died suddenly but peacefully, like he was going to sleep. The family is heading to the hospital now."

The group was in shock, and it seemed as if everything was happening in slow motion. "I guess it's time for me to communicate what Grandpa told me to ask you if and when this day ever came," said Walt. "His final wish was that all of you would attend his funeral at our church as his special guests. As soon as I know the details, I will pass them along. He loved each one of you deeply and appreciated the impact you had on his life. It would mean a lot to me and our family if you all would come."

QUESTIONS FOR PERSONAL REFLECTION

1. On a scale of one to ten, how would you rate yourself on your level of diligence to study God's Word and apply it to your joys and struggles?

2. Is there evidence in your life that you believe God has called you to be a student? What steps could you take to live in a way that was more consistent with this aspect of your identity?

3. What do you make of Andy's analysis that sinful anger is sometimes a lazy approach to problem solving?

QUESTIONS FOR GROUP DISCUSSION

1. Discuss the relationship between being made in the image of God and his calling to be a lifelong learner.

2. Who stands out at your church as a longtime believer who has been a good steward of the learning opportunities the Lord has provided? What have you appreciated about this person?

3. Do you think most people in today's culture are inclined toward careful reflection or knee-jerk reactions? What trends do you see in culture that affect a Christian's willingness to learn slowly and methodically?

CHAPTER 30

You Are Going Home

Andy, Dee, Curt, Faye, and Pete met in the church parking lot about one-half hour before the memorial service. They had never been inside a predominately black church before and were somewhat apprehensive about how they would be received and what they might experience. However, they felt honored that Pastor Cummings had asked them to attend, and they knew he had specific reasons for doing so.

They were greeted at the door by a gray-haired man who introduced himself as Deacon Rawlings. "You must be Pastor's special guests that Walt told me about," he said. "We're grieving mightily right now because we loved our pastor dearly. But like he taught us so many times from that sacred desk, when a person dies in Christ, we don't have to sorrow as those who have no hope. Thank you for joining us to honor him and the Savior he adored."

Deacon Rawlings ushered them to a place that had been reserved for them in the middle of the packed auditorium. Walt was sitting near the front with his family, and when he saw the group sit down, he came back to greet them. "Grandpa would be honored that you are here," he said.

"We are so thankful he would want us to be here," said Faye.

"Grandpa thought a lot of each of you," Walt said. "He thoroughly enjoyed our studies together and felt like you treated him with dignity and respect."

"He was a powerful encouragement to us," said Andy. "I knew him for only a few months, and I know I am going to miss him terribly. I cannot imagine what this is like for you, your family, and your church family."

"When Grandpa asked me to invite you to the service, he did have one last message," Walt said with a glimmer in his eye.

Faye thought, *I've seen that glimmer before—in Pastor Cummings's eyes.*

"Grandpa said to tell you, 'Watch our church family. See if they believe.'"

The group sat silently as they wondered what Pastor Cummings meant by that cryptic statement. Like many things he had said to them during their times together, this message had been carefully crafted to pique their attention. As they waited for the service to start, they looked at the men and women seated around them, and they thought back to the stories Pastor Cummings had told about living as a black man in the United States.

They wondered how many of the people in the congregation had also been called mean-spirited racial slurs as a regular matter of course each day. Or how many had been denied a mortgage simply because of the color of their skin. Or how many had been victims of prejudice at school, work, or in their neighborhoods. The longer they sat, the less comfortable they became.

Pastor's statement "See if they believe" kept running through their minds. Had the men and women around them believed the callous messages the world had shouted at them? That their ethnicity determined their value and destiny? That they were substandard and ill-suited for polite society? That they were not worth civil treatment and fairness under the law? Had they chosen to define themselves by the world's opinion of their identity?

A booming voice jarred them out of their contemplation. "We've gathered to pay our final respects to our dear Pastor Everette Cummings and to share our condolences with each family member and friend. For those who don't know me, I'm Deacon Goodnight, and I'm the song-leader here. Now, most of you all are from this church, and you know what our Pastor taught us about days like this."

Several members of the congregation blurted out responses in a way that caught Andy, Dee, Curt, Faye, and Pete off guard. "Sorrow lasts for the night, but joy comes in the morning," one elderly woman proclaimed. "This world is not our home," affirmed a teenage male. That was followed by several "Amens!" Then a man shouted, "We'll see our pastor again!" A little girl jumped up and said, "Jesus is the way, the truth, and the life." The group had never seen anything quite like this, but the testimonies of faith in the power of Christ's resurrection brought strength to their hearts.

"Sounds like we have something to sing about," declared Deacon Goodnight. Instantly, the choir erupted into the first song and every-one was on their feet, singing, clapping, and dancing to the words. Other songs followed. Some were sad, and the music would slow down and the people would lower their voices. During these songs the sing-ing was mixed with weeping, like you might expect when a lament psalm was sung. Then came a song about the hope of heaven, and the exuberance was deafening. Before the group knew what was happen-ing, they were standing, singing, and swaying along with everyone else. The focus on Christ and the power of his death, burial, and resurrec-tion moved them deeply.

As they sang, the members of the group nodded at each other as if to say, "They believe. They truly believe what God says about them."

Next came a young black man who introduced himself as Pastor Blanchard, obviously the heir-apparent of Pastor Cummings's minis-try. He professed that he was somewhat nervous about the shoes God was calling him to fill. The church family sensed his grief and uneas-iness and helped him along by punctuating his funeral sermon with loud statements of "Amen!" "You know that's right," and "Give it to us, Pastor."

The young preacher recapped Pastor Cummings's fifty-plus years of ministry in their community. He touched briefly on their pastor's involvement in racial justice initiatives, community development, and other aspects of civic life. He also spoke of the trials and tragedies that attended life for a black man in a racially prejudiced society.

"But everyone here knows where our Pastor Cummings got his information about how to think of himself. Was it from this ol' world? Was it from his own accomplishments?" the young preacher asked. "Absolutely not," shouted one dear woman. "Never one time," added a deacon.

"Then where did our pastor turn to learn what to believe about himself?" asked Pastor Blanchard.

"From God's Word!" shouted several people together. "The good book," said another.

Pastor Blanchard then presented the gospel message and shared how Pastor Cummings's hope was in the finished work of Jesus Christ on the cross. The reason he was able to carry himself with dignity and grace was because he had chosen to believe what God's Word said about who he was in Christ. Pastor Blanchard then invited everyone present to test their hearts to be sure they, too, had trusted Christ's shed blood as their only hope of heaven.

The pastor then exhorted his church family, saying, "Tell us a verse of Scripture that can strengthen us right now." Person after person quoted passages from God's Word that Pastor Cummings had taught them over the years that spoke of the certainty of heaven, the sufficiency of Christ's sacrifice, and the new life available through Jesus' finished work.

After dozens of Bible verses had been shared, Pastor Blanchard pointed down to his beloved mentor's casket. "And where is our dear pastor now?" he asked.

"He's gone home to be with our sweet Jesus," one elderly woman said, "and someday we're going home too."

Yes, the dear people in this church had chosen to believe what God said about them.

QUESTIONS FOR PERSONAL REFLECTION

1. Read Ecclesiastes 7:2. Why do you think this passage says it is better to go to a memorial service than it is to go to a party?

2. What do you want people to be able to say about you and your beliefs at your memorial service?

3. What verses of Scripture come to mind when you contemplate the believer's eternal hope?

QUESTIONS FOR GROUP DISCUSSION

1. What passages can you find in God's Word that describe heaven as being a place where people of many ethnicities will join together to worship the Savior?

2. What memorable funerals have you attended over the years? What made them stand out?

3. What thoughts come to mind as you consider the fact that, in heaven, we will dwell together for all eternity with people from many ethnicities?

CHAPTER 31

What Do You Believe?

During our journey together these past thirty days, we've considered what the various members of our group chose to believe about different aspects of their lives. It truly is amazing to contemplate how much instruction we find in God's sufficient Word on this subject.

However, the ultimate question before us is this: What do *you* believe? There are many voices in our culture screaming messages from different perspectives. Often their goal is either to sell you a product or gain your adherence to a specific point of view. Regrettably, many of the ideas presented in today's world are the polar opposite of what God's Word calls you to believe.

The challenge to determine what you should believe is complicated by the beliefs and ideas you have accumulated over the years about who you really are. We all have been affected by a lifetime of experiences both good and bad. None of us are immune from adopting ideas about our identity that are simply untrue.

The goal of our time together has been to encourage you to examine carefully what you believe. Hopefully, just as each member of our fictitious group was challenged to reevaluate their beliefs each time they met, you, too, have had opportunities to reflect on what God says about you. As we near the end of this book, it's now time for you to give careful thought to the all-important question we've been asking: What do *you* believe?

ABOUT YOUR NEED OF A SAVIOR

The most important decision that any person will ever make is what they believe about Jesus Christ. Our self-righteous hearts tell us we can save ourselves in our own strength and wisdom. "I am not nearly as bad as the guy down the street," we tell ourselves. The world chips in the false notions that "Surely God will grade on a curve," or "A loving God would never send anyone to hell."

The list of potential wrong beliefs about your eternal destiny is stunning. Against that backdrop of error stands the simple but profound message of the gospel:

- "God so loved the world, that He gave His only begotten Son, that whoever believes in Him shall not perish, but have eternal life" (John 3:16).

- "If you confess with your mouth Jesus as Lord, and believe in your heart that God raised Him from the dead, you will be saved; for with the heart a person believes, resulting in righteousness, and with the mouth he confesses, resulting in salvation" (Romans 10:9-10).

- "In Him, you also, after listening to the message of truth, the gospel of your salvation—having also believed, you were sealed in Him with the Holy Spirit of promise, who is given as a pledge of our inheritance, with a view to the redemption of God's own possession, to the praise of His glory" (Ephesians 1:13-14).

- "For this reason I also suffer these things, but I am not ashamed; for I know whom I have believed and I am convinced that He is able to guard what I have entrusted to Him until that day" (2 Timothy 1:12).

If you have never admitted your sin and placed your trust in the death, burial, and resurrection of Jesus Christ, I would encourage you to pause and make that decision today. Doing this is as simple yet as profound as Paul's instructions to the Philippian jailer: "Believe in the Lord Jesus, and you will be saved" (Acts 16:31). The great news is that those who have made this decision can enjoy the assurance of their salvation. The apostle John affirmed, "These things I have written to you who believe in the name of the Son of God, so that you may know that you have eternal life" (1 John 5:13).

ABOUT YOUR IDENTITY IN CHRIST

Up till now I have chosen not to use this term because of my desire to keep this book as simple and understandable as possible, but what we have been discussing together is referred to in theological circles as the *gospel indicatives*. This term refers to all that the Bible says about who we are in Christ. Generally when you see this term, it is being used in contrast to the *gospel imperatives*—the commands we are to follow because of our salvation. In Scripture, the indicatives always precede the imperatives because our identity in Christ is what empowers us to obey joyfully. This is why, for example, before Paul wrote the important commands in Ephesians 4–6, he treated us to the treasure trove of truth about our identity in Christ in Ephesians 1–3.

The challenge for many of us is that we are more comfortable with the imperatives than the indicatives. "Tell me quickly what I am supposed to do," often goes down in our legalistic mindset easier than, "Encourage me slowly to contemplate who I am in Christ." That is why many of us are more familiar with the commands of Ephesians 4–6 than the identity-markers of Ephesians 1–3.

The goal of this book has been to help each of us *slow down and savor* what the Bible instructs us to believe about who we are in Christ. Even though we have devoted a month to this study, the truth is that in many ways we have just begun to scratch the surface. But hopefully by now you are motivated to challenge yourself to think carefully about what you believe about yourself. Now is the time to decide: What do you believe about your identity in Christ? And what adjustments should you make in your heart and life to bring these biblical truths more to the forefront of your mind when you look in the mirror each day?

ABOUT YOUR ETERNAL HOME

Pastor Cummings was a fictitious character, but it was still difficult for me to write about his death. Perhaps you experienced a similar sensation as you read about what happened to him and the memorial service. Isn't that strange? Yet perhaps this reveals something about our hearts. We do not like to think about our own mortality. Culture does everything possible to soften the blow of death, using terms like *passed away* or *passed on* instead of *death* and *dying*. However, the king of terrors will not be dismissed with such impotent efforts. Everyone needs to decide what he or she believes about their eternal destiny.

Thankfully, followers of Jesus Christ are blessed with a comprehensive set of truths regarding this subject. Deacon Rawlings was right when he said we sorrow, but not as those who have no hope (1 Thessalonians 4:13). The apostle Paul mocks death because of the overwhelming power of the resurrection of Jesus Christ:

> O death, where is your victory? O death, where is your sting? The sting of death is sin, and the power of sin is the law; but thanks be to God, who gives us the victory through our Lord Jesus Christ. Therefore, my beloved brethren, be steadfast, immovable, always abounding in the work of the Lord, knowing that your toil is not in vain in the Lord (1 Corinthians 15:55-58).

Ultimately, every person must decide what they believe will happen the moment they die. Jesus himself tenderly said as much to his friend Martha in the touching scene that took place at her brother Lazarus's tomb: "I am the resurrection and the life; he who believes in Me will live even if he dies, and everyone who lives and believes in Me will never die. Do you believe this?" (John 11:25-26).

That question is as relevant today as it was nearly 2,000 years ago.

Regarding all that God's Word says about who you are in Christ—*Do you believe this?*

QUESTIONS FOR PERSONAL REFLECTION

1. Of all the aspects of our identity in Christ that were explored in this book, which one was newest to you? Most important to you? Most impactful?

2. Of all the various aspects of your identity in Christ, which one or two would you most want to further apply to your life? Why those? How might you go about making that happen?

3. God's Word is for applying *and* for passing on. Who do you know that would benefit from learning these truths about their identity in Christ? In a natural, humble, and caring way, how could you begin to share some of these truths with that person (or persons)?

QUESTIONS FOR GROUP DISCUSSION

1. How has this study resulted in specific, practical changes in your life already?

2. As you think about the future, which aspect of your union with Christ needs to have a more prominent place in your thinking?

3. How and in what ways has your love for your Savior grown over the course of reading this book?

Bibliography

Baker, Amy. *Why Do I Care?: When Others' Approval Matters Too Much.* Greensboro, NC: New Growth Press, 2016.

Bainton, Roland. *Here I Stand: A Life of Martin Luther.* New York: Abingdon & Cokesbury, 1960.

Calvin, John. *Institutes of the Christian Religion.* Ed. John T. McNeil, trans. Ford Lewis. Philadelphia: Westminster, 1960.

Kruger, Melissa, ed. *Identity Theft: Reclaiming the Truth of Who We Are in Christ.* Wheaton, IL: Crossway, 2018.

Plantinga Jr., Cornelius. *Not the Way It's Supposed to Be.* Grand Rapids, MI: Eerdmans, 1995.

Priolo, Lou. *Self-Image: How to Overcome Inferiority Judgments.* Phillipsburg, NJ: P&R Publishing, 2007.

Spurgeon, Charles Haddon. "The Immutability of God," sermon number 1 in *Spurgeon's Sermons: Metropolitan Tabernacle Pulpit and New Park Street Pulpit* (63 vols.). Accordance edition, Oak-Tree Software, 2012.

Welch, Edward T. *What Do You Think of Me? Why Do I Care? Answers to the Big Questions in Life.* Greensboro, NC: New Growth Press, 2011.

———. *When People Are Big and God Is Small: Overcoming Peer Pressure, Codependency, and the Fear of Man.* Phillipsburg, NJ: P&R Publishing, 1997.

Notes

1. Cornelius Plantinga, Jr., *Not the Way It's Supposed to Be* (Grand Rapids, MI: Eerdmans, 1995), ix.

2. Roland Bainton, *Here I Stand: A Life of Martin Luther* (New York: Abingdon & Cokesbury, 1960), 49-50. Emphasis added.

3. John Calvin, *Institutes of the Christian Religion*, ed. John T. McNeil, trans. Ford Lewis (Philadelphia: Westminster, 1960), Institutes 1.11.8, 108.

4. Philippians 2:13.

5. Charles Haddon Spurgeon, "The Immutability of God," sermon number 1 in *Spurgeon's Sermons: Metropolitan Tabernacle Pulpit and New Park Street Pulpit* (63 vols.), Accordance edition, OakTree Software, 2012.

6. See 2 Peter 1:3.

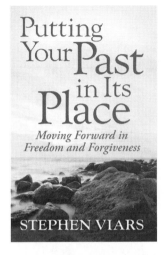

PUTTING YOUR PAST IN ITS PLACE

Lives grind to a halt when people don't know how to relate to their past. Some believe "the past is nothing" and attempt to suppress the brokenness again and again. Others miss out on renewal and change by making the past *more* important than their present and future. Neither approach moves people toward healing or hope.

Pastor and biblical counselor Stephen Viars introduces a third way to view one's personal history—by exploring the role of the past as God intended. Using Scripture to lead readers forward, Viars provides practical measures to

- understand the important place "the past" is given in Scripture
- replace guilt and despair with forgiveness and hope
- turn failures into stepping stones for growth

This motivating, compassionate resource is for anyone ready to review and release the past so that God can transform their behaviors, relationships, and their ability to hope in a future.

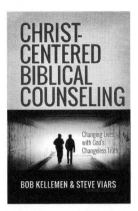

CHRIST-CENTERED BIBLICAL COUNSELING

Christ-Centered Biblical Counseling is a comprehensive resource that will help you understand how to minister from God's truth to change lives. With the cumulative wisdom of almost 40 contributors with exceptional credentials and experience, you'll discover a valuable model for counseling that explains...

The *Why* of Biblical Counseling

- *Why* the Bible is sufficient and relevant for addressing every issue we face

- *Why* biblical counseling is so effective in helping people face life's struggles in Christ's strength

The *How* of Biblical Counseling

- *How* you can lead struggling, hurting people to the hope and strength available only in Christ

- *How* to counsel in a way that is Christ-centered and God-glorifying

Every chapter provides a wonderful blend of theological wisdom and practical expertise, and is written to be accessible to everyone who wishes to extend Christ's love to others—pastors, church leaders, counseling practitioners, instructors, lay people, and students.

To learn more about Harvest House books and
to read sample chapters, visit our website:

www.HarvestHousePublishers.com

HARVEST HOUSE PUBLISHERS
EUGENE, OREGON